Comments on other *Amazing Stories* from readers and reviewers

"You might call them the non-fiction response to Harlequin romances: easy to consume and potentially addictive."
Robert Martin, *The Chronicle Herald*

"Tightly written volumes filled with lots of wit and humour about famous and infamous Canadians."
Eric Shackleton, *The Globe and Mail*

"This is popular history as it should be ... For this price, buy two and give one to a friend."
Terry Cook, a reader from Ottawa, on **Rebel Women**

"Stories are rich in description, and bristle with a clever, stylish realness."
Mark Weber, *Central Alberta Advisor*, on **Ghost Town Stories II**

"The resulting book is one readers will want to share with all the women in their lives."
Lynn Martel, *Rocky Mountain Outlook*, on **Women Explorers**

"[The books are] *long on plot and character and short on the sort of technical analysis that can be dreary for all but the most committed academic."*
Robert Martin, *The Chronicle Herald*

"A compelling read. Bertin ... has selected only the most intriguing tales, which she narrates with a wealth of detail."
Joyce Glasner, *New Brunswick Reader*, on **Strange Events**

"The heightened sense of drama and intrigue, combined with a good dose of human interest, is what sets Amazing Stories *apart."*
Pamela Klaffke, *Calgary Herald*

MURDER!

AMAZING STORIES®

MURDER!

The Mysterious Death of Canadian Mining Magnate Sir Harry Oakes

by Cheryl MacDonald

James Lorimer & Company Ltd., Publishers
Toronto

James Lorimer & Company Ltd., Publishers acknowledge the support of the Ontario Arts Council. We acknowledge the support of the Government of Canada through the Book Publishing Industry Development Program (BPIDP) for our publishing activities. We acknowledge the support of the Canada Council for the Arts for our publishing program. We acknowledge the support of the Government of Ontario through the Ontario Media Development Corporation's Ontario Book Initiative.

Library and Archives Canada Cataloguing in Publication

MacDonald, Cheryl, 1952-
Murder! : the mysterious death of canadian mining magnate Sir Harry Oakes / Cheryl MacDonald.

(Amazing stories)
ISBN 978-1-55277-407-6

1. Oakes, Harry, Sir, 1874-1943. 2. Murder — Bahamas.
I. Title. II. Series: Amazing stories (Toronto, Ont.)

HV6535.B33 N37 2009   364.152'3092   C2009-900450-X

James Lorimer & Company Ltd., Publishers
317 Adelaide Street West, Suite 1002
Toronto, Ontario
M5V 1P9
www.lorimer.ca

Printed and bound in Canada

Mixed Sources
Cert no. SW-COC-001271
© 1996 FSC

Contents

*Sir Harry Oakes, leaning against an airplane in Nassau,
Bahamas, on January 1, 1941.*

Prologue

The room smelled of smoke, charred flesh, and singed feathers. The lacquered finish on an ornately decorated Chinese screen had been charred and blistered by the heat. Curtains and rugs were scorched; over one of the single beds, blackened mosquito netting hung in ruins.

On the bed lay the mortal remains of Sir Harry Oakes, the richest baronet in the British Empire. Behind his left ear were four deep triangular wounds. Blood had seeped across his face, which was black with soot. His pajamas had been partly destroyed by flames. His neck, chest, groin, left knee, and right foot were covered with blisters.

Someone had killed Harry Oakes, then tried to hide the murder by dousing the bed with gasoline or some other flammable substance and setting it ablaze. The mattress still smoked, but the worst of the fire had been drowned by a heavy tropical storm blowing in through the open window. An electric fan still turned at the foot of the bed, blowing cool air onto the corpse. The artificial breeze stirred dozens of feathers that were stuck to the blisters and blood covering the corpse.

"Hi, Harry," called a voice from the veranda. Harold

Murder!

Christie, Sir Harry's business partner and house guest, was ready for breakfast with his friend.

There was no reply.

Harold Christie opened the door and walked into a nightmare.

The deathbed of Sir Harry Oakes behind the scorched Chinese screen at the scene of the murder.

Chapter 1
The Millionaire Miner

S ir Harry Oakes was born plain Harry Oakes in Sangerville, Maine, on December 23, 1874. His father, William Pitt Oakes, was a civil engineer, and his mother, Edith, was a temperance advocate. The Oakes family lived in very comfortable circumstances. At a time when thousands of North Americans could not afford high school, Harry and his brother, Louis, attended Foxcroft Academy, a prestigious private secondary school established in 1823. Upon graduation, Harry went on to Bowdoin College in Brunswick, Maine, where he completed an arts degree. Then he enrolled at Syracuse Medical College with the intention of becoming a doctor.

Later, Harry would claim he dropped out when he learned how poorly doctors were paid. That may have been partly true. As a young man, Harry made it clear he wanted to amass a fortune. But restlessness likely also influenced his decision. In 1898, after hearing about the discovery of gold in the Klondike, he announced to his family that he was heading off in search of a bonanza. Harry's family stood squarely behind his impetuous decision. His mother provided him with a bit of money. His brother promised to send him something from the lumber business he was just starting. And his sister, Gertrude, offered to send whatever she could spare from her secretarial job.

Their confidence must have provided Harry with some comfort as he alternately froze and sweated in his search for gold. He travelled thousands of kilometres, enduring terrible weather, primitive living conditions, bad food, and worse company. But there was no fabulous wealth awaiting Harry in the Canadian northwest. Like thousands of other gold-seekers, he found only disappointment. Most of these gold-seekers eventually returned to civilization and regular jobs. However, a handful surrendered completely to gold fever, eagerly soaking up reports of new gold strikes and heading off to try their luck again and again.

Harry Oakes was one of these. After the Klondike, he went to Nome, Alaska, where his luck as a prospector was equally poor. Australia was next. Harry worked his way there, paying for his passage with a stint as a ship's purser. Then it was on to New Zealand, where he supported himself for a while as a government surveyor. Harry also tried farming

Sir Harry Oakes

and did very well raising flax — so well, in fact, that within two years he had put aside £30,000. That might have been the foundation for a successful career in agriculture, but Harry was not interested. He used the money to return to mining, first in Death Valley, California, then back in Alaska, then in the Belgian Congo.

The prospecting life rapidly scoured away whatever veneer of gentility Harry had acquired during his childhood and adolescence. He learned to drink and curse, to size up a man's character quickly, to guard his own back, to fight when necessary. Although many miners formed partnerships with a mind to mutual protection and division of labour, relatively few of these relationships blossomed into lasting friendships. The elusive sparkle of gold was always there, a palpable presence that could not be ignored. And, in Harry's case, friendships were even more difficult to sustain because of his foul temper. He could be loyal, kind, and generous, but he could be just as stubborn, opinionated, and given to loud and lengthy bursts of anger. Even in calmer conversations, he had an annoying habit of whistling under his breath or shuffling his feet, making some people think he was mentally unbalanced. He was also vindictive, going to great lengths to get revenge if he felt he had been wronged.

By 1911, he was 36 years old, strong, and stocky at a height of just 5 feet 6 ½ inches. His red hair was a bit faded and beginning to recede. His brown eyes were still keen and sharp. But all he had to show for 13 years of hard work was a collection of colourful stories, which he loved to tell again and again. One such story recounted how Harry and a partner were prospecting in Alaska when their boat was blown off course. They landed in Siberia and were promptly arrested by Cossacks. Another time he crawled into a cool cave in Death Valley to sleep through the hottest part of the day, only to discover when he awoke that he was sharing the cave with a nest of rattlesnakes.

Harry had also acquired considerable mining experience and knowledge of geology. He was convinced that, sooner or later, his knowledge would pay off. So, when he heard of lucrative strikes in northern Ontario, he decided to scope out the territory.

On June 19, 1911, he arrived in Swastika, Ontario, about eight kilometres (five miles) southwest of Kirkland Lake. Why he chose that particular location has become a matter of legend. According to one story, Harry looked at a map and picked the spot at random. Another story says he was thrown off a train because he couldn't pay his fare. A third version claims he was on his way to Kapuskasing when he fell into conversation with another passenger, a miner named George Tough. The bottle of Scotch the two men had been sharing wasn't quite empty when they reached Swastika, so Harry got off the train to help George finish it. Whatever the truth, Harry was close to broke. He had only $2.65 in his pocket, but he was still determined to find his fortune. So he went into a partnership with George and George's brothers, Tom and Jack.

Harry's approach to prospecting was comprehensive. He analyzed every bit of geological information he could find. He scouted likely locations around Swastika and Kirkland Lake, looking for promising sites. He also did background research, checking through records of previous claims. George Tough did the same. There had been some significant strikes in the area, including a lucrative mine established by Bill Wright. When George Tough learned that title to several claims, including Wright's, would expire in January 1912, he formed a bold plan. Late one night, George, his brothers, and Harry Oakes got out of bed. The temperature was -47° Celsius (-52°

Fahrenheit). Harry pulled on five pairs of pants to protect himself from the frigid weather. Then the men walked out into the darkness. Within a few hours they had staked their claims to 11 sites. Bill Wright, who reached his claim at 4 a.m. — four hours after the deadline — was out of luck.

The shrewdly aggressive strategy quickly paid off. Two rich veins were discovered by the owners of Tough-Oakes Gold Mines. But Harry was still not satisfied. Production was inconsistent, and besides, he had to share the profits with the Tough brothers. He looked around for other possibilities and, in partnership with Ernie Martin, checked out the south shore of Kirkland Lake.

Ernie found gold in July 1912. The site looked promising, so Harry filed two claims and took an option on a third. Then began the hard work of developing the mine, which Harry and Ernie called Lake Shore. Money was required for equipment, supplies, and transportation, and although there was the potential for becoming very wealthy, neither Harry nor Ernie had the necessary start-up cash. Still, Harry was so convinced that Lake Shore was the mine he had been seeking for the past 14 years that he decided to dissolve his partnerships with the Tough brothers and Ernie. He asked family and friends for help, giving them shares in exchange for cash or credit. Since he had problems convincing wealthy backers to invest, he sent a friend, Clem Foster, to England to sell shares.

Foster did his job well, but he also skimmed off a commission — without telling Harry. When Harry found out, he had Clem charged with fraud. It took seven years, but Harry won his case in 1921. He promptly printed several thousand copies of the judgment and sent it to everyone he knew.

By this time, Harry was a rich man. Lake Shore proved to be one of the highest-producing gold mines in the world, second only to William Randolph Hearst's Homestake Mine in South Dakota. Everyone who had accepted shares in the mine was wealthy, including Harry's mother, his brother, and his sister, Gertrude, who moved to northern Ontario to work as Harry's personal assistant. Wealth also brought considerable power, which Harry regularly abused by getting even with people who had slighted him during the long, lean years. Among his targets was store owner Jimmy Doige, who had embarrassed Harry when he tried to buy overalls on credit. After Harry forbade his employees to shop at Doige's store, the business went under and Doige left town.

Years later, a situation occurred that illustrates the two sides of Harry Oakes's personality. Doige was nearing the end of his life, and he was in financial difficulties. When someone told Harry about Doige's precarious situation, Harry growled, "Serves the bastard right," then he told his secretary to send Doige a cheque for $10,000.

Whether Harry was trying to salve a guilty conscience or buy friendship with his impulsive generosity is difficult to say. He frequently gave to worthy causes and entertained lavishly. He desperately wanted to be accepted by the most wealthy and powerful members of society. However, while he could afford to live like a gentleman, he found it impossible to shake off the habits acquired as a prospector. He took up golf, still very much a game for the affluent middle class, but he continued to swear and drink. His manners were atrocious: at meals, he frequently ignored his fork and ate only with his knife. He was also known to spit grape seeds or fruit pits across the room during formal dinners. And his temper was as violent as ever. Harry Oakes, the millionaire miner, had plenty of acquaintances, but few friends.

In 1922, with the case against Clem Foster settled and Lake Shore bringing in tremendous profits, Harry decided to embark on a world cruise. He revisited some of the places he had seen as a miner, but this time he travelled first class. On board the ship he met Eunice McIntyre, a blue-eyed Australian girl of 22. Eunice was the daughter of a civil servant. At nearly 5 feet 10 inches, she was 3 inches taller than Harry; she was also gentle and easygoing — a perfect complement to Harry's volatile nature. They fell in love and married in Sydney in 1923.

Initially, Harry and Eunice lived at the Chateau, the one-and-a-half-storey log house Harry had built in Kirkland Lake in 1919. Constructed on an outcrop of solid rock, it was so close to Lake Shore that Harry could see the mine from his back porch. But Kirkland Lake was too much of a backwater for the newlyweds, especially after Eunice became pregnant. In 1924, the Oakes family moved to Niagara Falls. Harry bought a $500,000 mansion from Paul Schoellkopf, president of the Niagara Falls Power Company. Located on an eight-hectare (20-acre) estate at the top of Clark Hill, the house had a fine view of Dufferin Island, but was not quite up to Harry's standards. Over the next four years he had it renovated to include 35 rooms, 17 bathrooms, and air conditioning — a rare luxury in the 1920s. The estate, which Harry named Oak Hall, also included a swimming pool and a five-hole golf course. By the time Harry and Eunice moved into the mansion in 1928, they had two children: Nancy, born in May 1924, and Sydney, born in June 1927. By 1932, there would be three more: Shirley, William, and Harry Jr.

Harry, Eunice, and the children led a privileged life, travelling extensively between their houses in Niagara Falls; Bar Harbor, Maine; Palm Beach, Florida; London, England; a hunting lodge in Sussex, England; and the Chateau in Kirkland Lake. While his children attended the best schools, Harry took care of business and became increasingly involved in charity and community projects.

In 1930, he offered 16 acres of farmland at the corner of Stanley Avenue and Morrison Street to the City of Niagara Falls for use as a park and athletic field. It opened to the public in 1931. When the Clifton House Hotel burned in 1932, he bought the property specifically to block development. He also acquired another nearby hotel — the Lafayette — then donated both properties to the Niagara Parks Commission. Oakes Garden opened in 1937.

Meanwhile, Harry, who loved trees and green spaces, served on the Niagara Parks Commission and also created make-work projects to help unemployed residents of Niagara Falls during the desperate years of the Great Depression. One of the projects was the restoration of a historic section of Portage Road, which had been closed to accommodate the Canadian Southern Railroad. Harry paid workers $2 for a half-day's work. It was a pretty good wage for the times, but was even more notable because Harry insisted that all the workers be paid in two-dollar bills. The road was later named Oakes Drive.

These and other philanthropic gestures made Harry well-known in Niagara Falls and beyond, although he was still not particularly well-liked. Nor did his financial contributions to political parties make him popular in government circles. Harry made a practice of contributing to both the Liberals and the Conservatives, typically donating somewhat more to whichever party was in power in Ottawa. In 1930, as the Liberals prepared for a summer election, he was asked for a larger donation. He agreed, with the understanding that he would be appointed to the Senate when they won.

The Liberals were defeated and Harry lost his chance to become a senator. But worse things were in store. He was told that he would have to pay $25,000 in taxes on land he had donated to the Niagara Parks Commission. According to one biographer, Geoffrey Bocca, "He clutched his throat, found it impossible to breathe, and took to his bed, wheezing, choking, and gasping." The doctor diagnosed it as a severe bronchial attack, but in retrospect it seemed more likely a psychosomatic reaction. Harry, who had always been sensitive to slights, was convinced that R. B. Bennett's Conservative government was deliberately persecuting him, especially after he learned that the government was planning to increase taxes on the highest-producing mines. Harry was already paying a fortune in taxes. According to his estimate, by 1934 he was pouring over $17,500 *per day* into government coffers.

Harry had become a Canadian citizen in 1915, during World War I, at a time when the United States was still neutral. But he was thoroughly disenchanted with Canadian tax laws, and nothing could convince him to remain in his adopted country. In 1934, several months before the Canadian government implemented new tax laws, Harry Oakes moved his family out of the country.

Chapter 2
The Promoter and the Prince

Harry Oakes could afford to live anywhere in the world. He already owned several houses and any one of these could have become his official residence. Instead, he chose to move to Nassau, the capital of the Bahamas. He was greatly influenced in this decision by Harold Christie, one of three men who would play a significant role in Harry's last days and in the investigation of his murder.

Harold Christie was a wheeler-dealer — a real estate agent and tourism promoter who had big dreams for Nassau and the Bahamas. He spent a great deal of his time visiting the playgrounds of the rich and famous, including Palm Beach, Florida, where he tried to convince residents that the best place to enjoy themselves was the Bahamas. On one

Harold Christie & The Duke of Windsor

visit to Palm Beach, he learned that Harry Oakes was in town. Christie arranged a meeting, hoping to persuade Harry to invest in some of his schemes.

The meeting went well, although Christie soon realized that Harry was a shrewd businessman who could not be bamboozled by get-rich-quick schemes or elaborate but impractical dreams. However, Harry was also a great advocate of progress. He was intrigued by the developments Christie envisioned, including a tourist resort and airport.

What really persuaded Harry to move to the Bahamas and join forces with Harold Christie, though, was the news that Bahamian citizens were not required to pay income tax. By the time Christie left Palm Beach, Harry had asked him to arrange for Bahamian citizenship and to find him the best house available.

Westbourne became the Oakes family's tropical home. A long, rambling pink stucco building, the mansion boasted 20 rooms. Outside, the ground floor featured a walkway screened in with latticework on which grew bougainvillea and other tropical flowers. Above the walkway was the second-storey veranda, which ran the length of the house. Located on the edge of the Bahamas Country Club, Westbourne was within walking distance of the club's tennis courts and just a short drive from downtown Nassau.

Nassau was the largest town on New Providence Island, one of a cluster of islands, cays, and rocks that form the Bahamas. To some extent, the area's reputation as a tropical paradise was deserved. The sea was a beautiful, ever-changing expanse of blue and green. Lush vegetation and brilliant tropical flowers grew in profusion. But the soil was generally poor, and fresh water was often difficult to find. Generations of Bahamians had managed to eke out a living by turning to the sea, not just for fish and sponges, but also for piracy and salvage. A streak of lawlessness ran through the islands' past, a tradition of breaking the rules in pursuit of profit. In the twentieth century, the most notable example of this was a result of Prohibition. Florida was just 50 miles away, and many Bahamians made tidy profits by engaging in the sale and transportation of vast quantities of liquor, which were illegal in the United States. Harold Christie was one of them.

Christie had known poverty in his early years. His father was a talented and intelligent man who had once worked as chief of advertising for General Electric in New York. However, the elder Christie was also a member of the Plymouth Brethren, a strict religious sect. Whenever the spirit moved him, he would abandon his work and his family of eight children and spend weeks preaching on the small islands around Nassau. At times, the family was so poor that the children had to beg for food. However, after his father's death, Christie's mother built up a business, exporting straw hats to Georgia. She also dabbled in real estate.

Christie had inherited his mother's business acumen along with his father's intelligence and ability to envision limitless possibilities. He was not particularly practical about paperwork or administration, but he was shrewd and determined to hold on to much of what he earned. One factor contributing to his success was his kindness. Because he knew what it meant to be poor, Christie was able to empathize with others. When locals ran into problems, he helped out with generous loans of money, often accepting an option to buy small farms in return. Most of the farms were worth very little on their own, but as time passed, Christie amassed such a number of them that he was recognized as one of the most

powerful landowners in the Bahamas. He also had a network
of connections throughout the Bahamas — men on every
island who owed him favours and kept him apprised of news
that might be useful to him.

By the time Harry Oakes moved to Nassau, Christie's
rum-running days were behind him.

Prohibition was over and the economy of the islands
was sliding downhill, although Christie's ambitious plans to
make the area a major tourist centre were just beginning to
gel. Harry recognized the huge potential in Christie's plans
and teamed up with him on several deals. Over the next few
years, he bought a hotel and built a golf course and an airport. His dissatisfaction with service at local hotels led him
to establish a school to train hotel workers. Meanwhile, he
planted trees and experimented with farming. And, realizing
that political power would make it easier for him to achieve
his goals, he became involved in local politics.

For Harry Oakes, this was not just a way to earn bigger
profits. Despite the rough-edged character he presented to
the public, Harry longed for prestige. Money was not enough
for him, nor was the celebrity that came with his vast mil-
lions. He had been seriously disappointed at not being made
a Canadian senator. Now, as a Bahamian citizen, he was
determined to do everything possible to increase his social
position. He began by getting himself elected to the House of
Assembly in 1938. There is little doubt that some behind-the-
scenes negotiation was involved.

Alfred Francis Adderley, a barrister and the first black member of the House of Assembly, was elevated to the Legislative Council, becoming the first black Bahamian to achieve this milestone. Then Thaddeus Augustus Toote, another black barrister and former member of the House of Assembly, withdrew his candidacy in the election to replace Adderley. The new candidate was Milo H. Butler, a black grocer with few political connections. At the July 4 election, Harry won easily, with 538 votes against Butler's 70. There were suspicions that Harry and his closest supporters had used money and influence to assure his election.

More honours were in store. Again, Harry used every bit of influence he had, along with sizeable amounts of money. In 1939, after donating half a million dollars to St. George's Hospital in London, he was given a baronetcy by King George VI. The title was hereditary and could not have been awarded had he remained a Canadian citizen, which may have been one of the reasons Harry chose to move to the Bahamas.

Sir Harry Oakes was by now the richest and most powerful man in Nassau, surpassing even Harold Christie, who had become a close friend. Sir Harry owned more property than anyone else. He was the biggest private employer, as well as the area's most generous benefactor. Everyone knew him or knew of him. He and Lady Eunice entertained lavishly at Westbourne whenever they were at home. Their guests were often the rich and powerful of several countries, including the former King Edward VIII of England.

Murder!

Sir Harry and Edward had first met in England in 1934, when Edward was still the Prince of Wales. The eldest son of King George V was a popular figure, a playboy prince noted for his easygoing charm. But Edward was also self-indulgent and not particularly bright. When his father died in 1936, Edward was involved with Wallis Warfield Simpson. Wallis had three strikes against her: she was a commoner, an American, and a divorcée. More than half a century before the Charles–Camilla scandal shook Britain's royal family, Edward's liaison rocked the empire to its foundations. At the time, divorce was rare — only the wealthiest people could afford it. And to have the head of the Church of England marry a divorced woman was unthinkable.

Although some felt that the king's decision to give up his throne for love was a deeply romantic gesture, others considered Edward a fool — too stubborn to wait for some kind of compromise arrangement, too stupid and selfish to put matters of state before his own desires. But relatively little was said in the media, at least within the British Empire. In the 1930s, it was considered highly inappropriate to criticize any member of the royal family.

As king, Edward was one of the richest men in the world. As Duke of Windsor — the title given to him following his abdication — he was still a millionaire, but not nearly as wealthy as he had been previously. After their marriage in France in 1937, Edward and Wallis would be continually worried about money, since they lived beyond their means.

Meanwhile, the Windsors presented a serious problem to the British government.

Edward had been groomed for leadership, for all the duties life as Prince of Wales and then King of England entailed. His marriage had created endless complications. His family and the British government were wary of his bad judgment, one notable example of which was a 1937 trip to Nazi Germany. The German trip, which included a 90-minute conversation with Adolf Hitler, created a huge controversy at home.

World War II began in 1939. Neither Edward nor Wallis was comfortable living in Britain, where they felt they had been deeply insulted. As the wife of the Duke of Windsor, Wallis could use the title duchess throughout the duke's lifetime. However, she had no official standing, nor would any children she might bear during the marriage. She had been born a commoner and she would remain one, which meant every woman in the royal family took precedence over her. Friends who understood the subtleties of Britain's social ladder were no longer as friendly as they once had been.

But Wallis was a strong, determined woman and Edward could be equally stubborn, especially when his wife pressured him to take action. Again and again, he demanded an improvement in Wallis's social status. Although it was a characteristically thoughtless concern during wartime, Edward petulantly continued his demands for special treatment for his wife and a posting for himself. Finally, British prime minister Winston Churchill offered him a position as Governor General of the Bahamas.

It was something of an insult. The Bahamas was a remote, unimportant colony, far from the sophisticated cities Edward and Wallis preferred, and of little real significance when it came to the war effort. But Edward was backed into a corner. So, on a humid afternoon in mid-August 1940, he and Wallis sailed into Nassau. The heat was so intense that Edward's khaki uniform was quickly soaked with sweat, and the signature on the documents making him Governor General was smeared by perspiration that dripped from his face.

The Windsors hated Nassau. Government House, the official residence of the Governor General, was musty, run down, and badly decorated. The Bahamian House of Assembly had voted £1,500 to improve and redecorate Government House, but it wasn't nearly enough money to pay the fees of the New York decorator Wallis hired. Within a very short time, the budget had exceeded £5,000. Although the House of Assembly paid the bill, they were not happy. Nor were they happy with Edward's insistence on drawing his official salary. Most Governor Generals had turned the money back into the national coffers. Edward would not — he needed it to maintain his lavish lifestyle.

Their mutual love of the good life was something Sir Harry and Edward had in common. Sir Harry, of course, was delighted to be hobnobbing with former royalty, while Edward, who had spent some happy times on his Alberta ranch, admired the rough-and-ready types that Sir Harry epitomized. In addition, they shared a concern for the development of the island, not simply bringing in rich tourists or residents, but also providing adequate schooling, health care, and housing for the majority of Bahamians who lived in poverty.

The former miner and the one-time king also shared a preoccupation with money. By the early years of World War II, the production of Lake Shore mine had dropped. In addition, Sir Harry had spent huge sums on charitable endeavours and other projects. Although he was far from impoverished, his estate had diminished considerably since the glory days of the 1920s and 1930s. Similarly, the abdication had greatly lessened Edward's financial resources. Finally, wartime restrictions on the movement of currency in and out of British territory made it difficult for both men to access what wealth they had.

However, Sir Harry and the Duke were used to getting their own way. Along with Harold Christie, they formed a business partnership with a Swedish multimillionaire named Axel Wenner-Gren, who arranged for money transfers through a Mexican bank. The transactions were illegal, but that did not bother Sir Harry, the Duke, or Harold Christie. Nor did they worry much about Wenner-Gren's unsavoury reputation.

The Swedish businessman had connections all over the world, notably in Nazi Germany. Although Sweden was officially neutral, Wenner-Gren was under surveillance by both British and American intelligence agencies, with good reason. Aside from laundering money for the Nazis, Wenner-Gren was also an active munitions dealer. Rumours abounded concerning his activities on Hog Island, opposite Nassau. In addition to being the site of the Swede's magnificent mansion, Shangri-la, this island was also the location of some suspicious activity. Several hundred workers, who were ostensibly engaged in farming there, had also built a small landing strip and dug canals that, it was rumoured, were deep enough to allow U-boats to enter. As well, Wenner-Gren's yacht, the *Southern Cross*, was equipped with a suspiciously large number of antennas and huge fuel tanks. The yacht could easily provide information and fuel for German U-boats in the vicinity of the Bahamas.

Displaying his characteristic lack of judgment, the Duke of Windsor was friendly with Wenner-Gren. In December 1940, Wallis suffered from an infected tooth and was unwilling to trust Bahamian dentists. When Wenner-Gren offered to take the Windsors to Miami on the *Southern Cross*, the couple agreed. Although it was technically a private visit, upon their arrival, the Windsors were greeted by a number of armed motorcycle police, who formed their bodyguard. British prime minister Winston Churchill was livid. He warned Edward that, while it was perfectly acceptable to cruise around the Caribbean, it was *not* acceptable to associate with a known enemy collaborator. Edward ignored the message and continued to associate with Wenner-Gren.

So did Sir Harry Oakes. At one point, he entertained the Swede's influential Mexican friend, General Maximinio Avila Camacho — brother of the president of Mexico. Camacho was greedy, acquisitive, and dangerous. When he arrived in Nassau with an entourage of 16, he first visited Westbourne. Then he asked to meet the Duke of Windsor, so Sir Harry quickly arranged it, without consulting any of the officials who should have been involved. Edward welcomed the Mexicans to Government House, even though they were all in Nassau illegally. Just prior to World War II, Mexico had seized British assets, leading to a break in diplomatic relations. Once more, the former king demonstrated his inability to grasp the sensitivities of wartime politics.

But then, Edward, like many in the upper crust of Bahamian society, had a well-defined sense of entitlement. The Duke of Windsor, Sir Harry, and Harold Christie were just three of many who ignored wartime regulations, long-standing laws, and social proprieties. They got away with it because the authorities who were supposed to enforce these regulations were often their friends and colleagues, part of the same social set.

The situation was very different if one was regarded as an outsider or a troublemaker. One man who fit this description was Alfred de Marigny, a dashing young playboy who soon learned the price of not fitting in. Ironically, de Marigny was destined to become Sir Harry Oakes's son-in-law.

Chapter 3
The Playboy

reddie de Marigny was tall, dark, and handsome. He was born Marie Alfred de Fouquereaux in Mauritius, off the coast of Africa, on March 29, 1910. He was the son of a sugar planter who was heir to a title that went back to pre-Revolutionary French aristocracy. When Freddie was three, his mother left his father for another man, whom she later married. Freddie's father effectively abandoned him to the care of relatives and servants, who never mentioned his mother or her scandalous behaviour. Freddie grew up believing she was dead.

Freddie was stunned when, in his late teens, he met her on a tennis court. When he confronted his family with the information, his father told him he wanted nothing to do

Freddie de Marigny & Nancy Oakes

with the woman who had abandoned him in 1913, and told Freddie to choose between the two of them. Freddie broke with his emotionally distant father, adopting his mother's surname — de Marigny — as his own.

French, African, Indian, and British cultures blended on the exotic tropical island in the Indian Ocean. Freddie absorbed aspects from each of these cultures, as well as a love of the sea. By the time he was in his late teens, he had also begun to acquire a taste for wealth, luxury, and female companionship, encouraged by his cousin and close friend Georges de Visdelou Guimbeau. Both of them had titles —

Murder!

Freddie was the Count de Marigny, while Georges was a marquis. However, the ancient titles came with little financial compensation, although Freddie did inherit some family money. Realizing that the tiny British colony was too small and remote to fulfill their ambitions, the two young men gravitated to London, England, which was then experiencing its final glory as the social, cultural and financial centre of the western world.

For a time, Freddie studied economics in London. Georges also dabbled at studies. But both were far more interested in money and social status than in scholarship. They worked, when they had to, in positions requiring well-dressed, affable individuals with excellent manners. Freddie also made a small fortune in the stock market, which he quickly spent. But much of their time was spent escorting wealthy young women to various social events. This brought them into continual contact with rich, powerful individuals. It also provided opportunities for romance, whether mild flirtations or more serious liaisons.

In Freddie's case, it led to marriage to Lucie Cohen, the daughter of a wealthy banker. The 1936 marriage was a disaster from the beginning. For their honeymoon, they planned a cruise to the United States. Freddie later recalled that Lucie would not go unless his cousin Georges accompanied them. He described the voyage as something out of one of Noel Coward's musical comedies, with the bride sharing her bed with both her husband and his cousin. The marriage ended a few weeks after the newlyweds arrived in New York.

Freddie easily shrugged off the marital mishap. He made many new friends in the United States, most of whom were people of wealth and influence. Among them were Coster and Ruth Schermerhorn. Coster was a senior partner in a brokerage firm founded by Ruth's wealthy family, the Fahnestocks. Ruth was a stunning, green-eyed blond. She and Freddie became lovers. Then, without warning, Ruth left her husband and young daughter and announced to Freddie that she was divorcing Coster so they could marry. Freddie reluctantly agreed to become engaged.

Freddie and Ruth married in November 1937. Using Ruth's substantial wealth, they purchased land on Eleuthera, a small island in the Bahamas, where they built a home, acquired a boat, and settled down to a life of luxury. Freddie spent so much time sailing that Ruth complained he was married to his boat. He promptly christened the sailboat *Concubine*, shocking many of the more strait-laced Bahamians.

They were equally shocked when Freddie and Ruth divorced in early 1940. As the wife of a British subject, Ruth was required to obey wartime currency regulations. This severely limited her access to cash. Freddie pointed out that if they divorced, she would no longer be subject to the regulations. She could get all the money she needed, and after the war was over, they could remarry. Ruth agreed. After the divorce, she continued to finance Freddie's ventures, which

included a grocery store, a beauty salon, apartment build-
ings, and a chicken farm.

Unlike many members of the Bahamas' elite, Freddie
could and did work hard when he needed to. But he also
enjoyed socializing. Because Bahamian society was very
small, he inevitably encountered the Windsors. He had actually met the Duke in England in 1932, a meeting Edward
remembered when he again encountered Freddie aboard
Axel Wenner-Gren's yacht, the *Southern Cross.*

At first it seemed the casual introduction might lead to
friendship in the Bahamas. Freddie was certainly impressed
with Wallis, whose grace and sense of style he admired.
Wallis was also impressed by the handsome Mauritian, and
he became a frequent guest at Government House. In time,
though, the young playboy and the Duke clashed. Supported
by his wife's money, his confidence in his own abilities and
charm, and an increasingly cynical attitude, Freddie took a
certain delight in upsetting the status quo. His devilry did not
endear him to the former king.

After joining the Royal Nassau Sailing Club, Freddie
entered the King's Cup Regatta. He won the first two races,
and it seemed likely he was going to win the third. Then a
friend informed him it was customary to allow the Governor
General to win the cup. "To hell with that," Freddie replied.

When word got out, he was called upon by club officials,
who said they had heard rumours that the mast of his sailboat
was hollow. If this was so, he would be disqualified. Freddie

denied it, challenging the delegation to drill holes in the mast and see for themselves. However, he made it clear that he expected a letter of apology when they found out his mast was as solid as that of any of the other boats. The men conferred briefly, then told him that they could not possibly write such a letter. Freddie refused to let them examine the mast.

After talking to his lawyer, Godfrey Higgs, Freddie realized he had no choice but to return the trophies he had already won and leave the club. If he withdrew from the race to make a point, the Governor General would win. If he entered and won, someone would certainly make a complaint. Freddie returned the trophies, resigned, and then joined the Nassau Yacht Club.

At that point, the yacht club had a charter but little else. After Freddie joined, the best and liveliest young sailors became involved, and they had a wonderful time. Many went on to compete in various races in the Bahamas and elsewhere. But they also managed to shock their elders by racing on a Sunday. Many Bahamians were members of the Plymouth Brethren, who believed Sunday should be a day of rest, not a time to indulge in sport or other frivolities.

Meanwhile, Freddie managed to offend the Duke of Windsor on at least two other occasions. After building his house on Eleuthera, Freddie decided to pipe water to a nearby impoverished village, where drinking water was in short supply. He paid for the pipes, a reservoir, and a windmill to provide power. The House of Assembly approved the project. All that was required was the Governor General's signature. Edward delayed because his friend Rosita Forbes had approached Freddie and complained about the lack of fresh water at her own house. Freddie had suggested she install gutters and a cistern. That was not the answer Rosita wanted; she felt that she, not the villages, should benefit from Freddie's plan. When Freddie confronted Edward about the situation, the duke pointed out that the villagers had done without a regular supply of fresh water up to that point, and could continue to do so. Freddie responded angrily. Edward stood up, indicating that the discussion was over. Freddie refused to leave. He pointed out that Edward was the Governor General of the Bahamas because Britain considered it an insignificant colony. Then he called Edward a "pimple on the ass of the British Empire."

The second instance involved a large quantity of very good cognac being sold at discount prices following a warehouse fire. Edward was interested in buying some, because cognac was difficult to obtain during World War II. However, one of Freddie de Marigny's friends arranged for the announcement of the sale to be buried in an obscure corner of the local paper. Freddie was able to purchase several cases before Edward was aware the sale had taken place.

A short time later, Edward sent Captain Wood to visit Freddie. Wood explained that the Duke had hoped to get some cognac and asked if Freddie could spare two cases. Freddie replied that they were not for sale.

"You did not expect that His Royal Highness would *buy* them, did you, old chap?" Wood asked in astonishment. When Freddie suggested that he might part with two cases, for £250 each, Captain Wood left. Some time later, Freddie sent two bottles to Government House, along with his card. Although Edward acknowledged the gift, thereafter relations between the men were strained. Freddie's behaviour had made it clear that he was not impressed by royalty, and especially not by the Duke of Windsor.

While no direct evidence exists, it is possible one of the sources of friction between Freddie and Edward had to do with Wallis. The Windsor marriage was under considerable strain and Wallis was bored in the Bahamas. She was wealthy, sophisticated, graceful, fashionable — all qualities Freddie admired. And Freddie vaguely resembled Felipe Espil, one of Wallis's former lovers. While Freddie may not have engaged in a full-blown affair with the Duchess of Windsor, they were both inclined to serious flirtation. Perhaps it was with Wallis's urging that Edward came to Freddie's rescue in early 1942.

Freddie's businesses were doing well, but his lifestyle was excessively lavish. In January 1942, he was charged with breaking currency regulations. He was ordered to appear before the Exchange Control Board to explain where he was getting his money.

It was a serious charge, serious enough to require Freddie to hire a lawyer. But it was Freddie's own chutzpah that resulted in the dismissal of the charges. Eric Hallinan, attorney general of the Bahamas, chaired the hearing before a number of officials. The Governor General was not directly involved, but as he did on numerous occasions, he sat off to the side, watching the proceedings. Early on, Freddie tossed an envelope on the table beside his lawyer. It was large, heavily stuffed, sealed, and across it in large red letters were the words, "Affidavits re. Expenses, Presents, etc."

The writing was clearly visible to members of the control board. When Freddie was asked where he was getting his money, he explained that he received substantial gifts from women friends, many of whom were lonely and enjoyed his company. Moreover, he could prove it with affidavits.

His revelation shocked the staid, strait-laced members of the control board, but the Duke of Windsor smiled. "It is clear to me that Mr. de Marigny has no reason to invent such a story of such a delicate nature," Edward remarked. Freddie was allowed to go without opening the envelope. Later, in his lawyer's office, Freddie opened the envelope and dumped out dozens of sheets of blank paper. Higgs's initial amusement quickly turned to anger. He warned Freddie that he had made fools of Hallinan and other members of the control board, and it was only a matter of time before they would get even. Freddie shrugged it off. He was accustomed to being at odds with the Nassau establishment.

His French accent, many love affairs, and cavalier dismissal of social traditions made Freddie a thorn in the side of Nassau society. But it also made him a dashing, almost piratical

figure to certain members of the younger generation, including Nancy Oakes. By the time she was in her mid-teens, Sir
Harry's oldest child had a huge crush on Alfred de Marigny.

Some people thought Nancy a spoiled brat. It was also
rumoured that she had a bad temper, like her famous father.
There was definitely a family resemblance. Nancy had her
father's auburn hair, along with deep-set eyes. But she was far
more sophisticated than her parents had been in their teens.
This was hardly surprising, since she had been in English
and European boarding schools since the age of 10. She had
begun dating at 14 and had travelled widely. She knew what
power and money could buy. And, like her father, Nancy was
accustomed to getting her own way.

According to Freddie de Marigny's memoirs, he first
met Nancy in 1939, when she was about 15. She was a freckle-
faced kid; he was in his late 20s and paid little attention to
her. She, on the other hand, was very interested in him and
she made her feelings clear right from the start. According to
Freddie, when his divorce from his second wife became final,
his cousin and close friend Georges de Visdelou suggested
he marry Nancy. Freddie could certainly use her fortune. But
Freddie was not interested.

Nancy grew into an attractive young woman. When
they met again at a party a couple of years later, Nancy was
wearing blue and white chiffon, and Freddie was struck by
how lovely she looked. Nancy told him she was unhappy at
home. She claimed her parents did not understand her, that

her mother was too bossy and her father was a boor. She felt stifled at home.

Nonetheless, they did not see each other again until Freddie was in a New York hospital in 1941, suffering from stomach pains. Seventeen-year-old Nancy, who was attending school in the city, visited him every day, bringing newspapers, fruit and other gifts.

At the 1941 Christmas Ball at Nassau's British Colonial Hotel, Nancy looked stunning in a green silk dress. After the first dance with her father, she grabbed Freddie's hand and led him to the dance floor. "Now I'm all yours," she told him. According to Freddie, they fell in love that night.

They saw each other whenever they could, both in the Bahamas and New York. Plenty of people knew about their relationship — except, apparently, Nancy's parents.

In the spring of 1942, they were both in New York City. Once more, Freddie was in the hospital. They began discussing marriage. Freddie was discharged on May 17, which was Nancy's 18th birthday. Two days later, without telling Nancy's family, they were married in a judge's chambers in the Bronx.

Sir Harry, Lady Eunice, and the younger children were vacationing in Bar Harbor, Maine, when Nancy called to tell her mother the news. Lady Eunice burst into tears. When she told Sir Harry what had happened, he was furious. After a few moments, though, he calmed down. "I suppose we had better make the best of it," he said. Then he asked to speak to Freddie.

"Tell me the truth," he demanded. "How much money

do you want?"

Freddie was insulted. "I have sufficient money to keep her and I will prove it to you."

For the time being, Sir Harry was happy with the answer. He told his new son-in-law he didn't care about what he had done in the past. From now on, though, he had better be good to Nancy.

To demonstrate their good will, Eunice paid for a Mexican honeymoon. The trip was a disaster. Nancy caught typhoid and had to be hospitalized. Her head was shaved — a standard treatment at the time — and she received several transfusions. Then she developed a serious gum disease, which required oral surgery. It was six weeks before she was able to leave the hospital.

The newlyweds joined the Oakes family in Palm Beach. Concerned about Nancy's health, Eunice gave her daughter and son-in-law separate rooms. Nancy was furious. At dinner in front of guests, she announced that it was too late for separate rooms; she was already pregnant.

Somehow, Sir Harry managed to control his legendary temper during the meal, but as soon as he could arrange it, he took Nancy to see a doctor. Given her age and health problems, the doctor recommended an abortion. Freddie was convinced his father-in-law had influenced the doctor's recommendation and said as much. But Nancy had decided that she was too young to have a baby. She did not want to be tied down, nor did she want to lose her figure, so she agreed to the abortion.

Nancy was in hospital for several weeks, during which time Freddie also checked in to have his tonsils removed. The couple had adjoining rooms. When Sir Harry discovered this, he was enraged. He accused Freddie of being a "sex maniac" and injuring his daughter's health. Freddie refused to get into an argument with his father-in-law, and Sir Harry calmed down.

After Nancy recovered, she and Freddie moved to a house in Nassau. Their relationship with Sir Harry improved somewhat, especially after Freddie informed his father-in-law that he had signed a paper giving up all rights to Nancy's money. At times, Sir Harry seemed to be developing a grudging respect for his son-in-law. Like Harry, Freddie was something of an adventurer, and he did not always play by the conventional rules of society. But he worked hard at the things that interested him, and he treated Nancy well.

Still, Sir Harry continued his curmudgeonly ways. On March 26, 1943, he dropped in to visit Nancy and Freddie. Things went well at first, but an argument broke out between the two men after Sir Harry had a few drinks. He was furious that Nancy and Freddie had turned down an invitation to Government House. They simply weren't interested, Freddie explained. Harry was disgusted, insisting it was important to associate with the right sort of people. Freddie shrugged. In spite of his fondness for luxury, Freddie had little patience with the more boring aspects of Nassau society. The argument became more personal, focussing on the de Marigny marriage and money. Freddie pointed out that he had never asked his father-in-law for anything; Sir Harry countered that he had provided everything Nancy had, including the clothes she wore. As Freddie escorted his father-in-law to the street, Sir Harry threatened to have him horsewhipped. In return, Freddie offered to "apply my big foot to his behind."

Three days later, Nancy threw a birthday party for Freddie. Among the guests was Nancy's younger brother, Sydney. When the party ended, Nancy invited Sydney to sleep over, and he accepted. Between four and five in the morning, the household was awakened by Sir Harry pounding on the door. He barged into the room where Sydney was sleeping. "Who gave you permission to sleep here?" he roared as he grabbed him by the ankle and pulled him out of bed. All the way to the car, he shouted insults at his 17-year-old son.

Sir Harry's temper was more than Nancy and Freddie were willing to tolerate. At one point Nancy wrote a letter threatening to break off all communication with her parents. She did not, partly because she still relied on them for various reasons, including school tuition. In any event, she was frequently away at school. Freddie, on the other hand, spent much of his time in Nassau, where it was possible to come into daily contact with Sir Harry, if he chose to do so. After Sir Harry pulled Sydney out of bed, Freddie avoided all contact with his father-in-law.

The next time he visited Westbourne, Sir Harry was dead.

Chapter 4
Murder in Paradise

Becuase July and August are unbearably hot and humid in the Bahamas, the Oakes family made a habit of escaping for a couple of months. By early July 1943, Lady Eunice and the younger children were at their summer home in Bar Harbor, Maine. Sir Harry was scheduled to fly out of Nassau on Friday, July 9.

On Wednesday, July 7, he invited friends for dinner at Westbourne. Charles Hubbard, Effie Henneage, and Harold Christie played tennis, drank cocktails, ate dinner, then had more drinks as they played Chinese checkers. Around 11, Hubbard and Mrs. Henneage left. Christie, who was one of Sir Harry's closest friends as well as a business associate, decided to stay overnight, something he did frequently. He

Murder scene with Oakes's half-burned body

had, in fact, slept at Westbourne the night before. Christie borrowed a pair of Sir Harry's brown silk pajamas and retired. His bedroom was just 20 feet from Sir Harry's, separated by a bathroom and small antechamber.

As Christie later recalled, both men were in their rooms shortly after 11. There was no one else in the house or on the grounds; the servants and watchmen had been given the night off. Although Sir Harry kept a pistol near him as he slept, all the doors were unlocked, as usual. The crime rate on New Providence Island was very low.

Around seven the following morning, Harold Christie

was ready for breakfast. He and Sir Harry usually ate together on the terrace overlooking the ocean. When he realized Harry was not yet up, Christie knocked on his door. There was no answer. He called out. Still no answer. Christie entered the master bedroom.

Horrible smells and sights assailed his senses. "For God's sake, Harry!" Christie shouted, when he saw his friend's charred and bloody body. He rushed to the bed, lifted Sir Harry's head, and placed a pillow under it. Then he took a glass of water and poured some into his mouth. The millionaire baronet was still warm, and it seemed to Christie that he swallowed some of the water. Christie rushed to the guest bathroom, wet a towel, then returned to wipe blood from his friend's face. Slowly, his mind absorbed the details of the horrific scene — the blisters, the blood, the feathers swaying slowly in the breeze created by the electric fan. Yet Christie thought there was still hope. He rushed outside and called for help.

No servants responded. The nearest cottage was occupied by Newell Kelly, manager of the Bahamas Country Club and a business associate of Sir Harry's. But Kelly was away on a fishing trip, and his wife Madeline did not hear Christie's cries for help. Christie telephoned her, asking her to send for a doctor and hurry to Westbourne. Next, Christie called his brother, Frank, whom he also asked to send a doctor. Finally he called Colonel R. A. Erskine-Lindop, commissioner of the Bahamas police force. When he was told Erskine-Lindop was not at home, Christie left a message with the commissioner's wife, then rushed back upstairs.

Madeline Kelly was the first to arrive. There was little she could do except offer Harold Christie moral support. Dr. Hugh Quackenbush reached Westbourne about 7:30. He knew immediately that Sir Harry was beyond help. On the side of his skull, just behind the left ear, were four triangular wounds. Probing one of the wounds, Dr. Quackenbush realized that Sir Harry's skull had been fractured. He guessed that he had been dead between two-and-a-half and five hours. As he examined the body, Dr. Quackenbush noticed that the mattress was still smouldering. He poured some water onto the bed.

In the meantime, Harold Christie had been back on the phone. At some point between 7 and 7:30, he called Government House and informed Major Gray Phillips, equerry to the Duke of Windsor, that Sir Harry Oakes was dead. Sir Harry and the duke had been scheduled to play golf together that day. However, golf was the furthest thing from the Duke of Windsor's mind after Major Phillips told him the news. No one can say precisely what he was thinking during the next couple of hours, but he spent a great deal of time contemplating his next move before taking action.

Meanwhile, Etienne Dupuch, a reporter and a member of the family that owned the *Nassau Tribune*, had telephoned Westbourne. Sir Harry had just imported a flock of sheep from Cuba, planning to raise them for meat, which was in short supply because of wartime rationing. Dupuch was supposed to interview him that morning, and was calling to confirm the appointment.

"He's dead!" Harold Christie blurted out when Dupuch identified himself.

"Who?" Dupuch enquired.

"Sir Harry. He's been shot!"

The violent death of a powerful and famous man was important news. After confirming that Sir Harry was indeed dead, Dupuch told Christie he would cable a report around the world.

By 9 a.m., the Duke of Windsor had reached some decisions. First of all, he decided that he would exercise his prerogative as Governor General and supervise all the details of the investigation. Second, he concluded that it was important to keep the story under wraps, at least during the initial investigation. Under the Emergency War Powers Act, he could censor any news coming out of the Bahamas, and this is what he intended to do concerning the death of Sir Harry Oakes. But that decision came too late. By the time Edward had chosen his course of action, the story was on the wires and Nassau was abuzz with rumours. Over the next several weeks, those rumours would change as bits of information became available and imaginations ran wild.

One of the rumours was that Sir Harry had been involved with a woman and had been killed by a jealous husband. The problem with that story was that Sir Harry was rather strait-laced about sexual matters and there was never any evidence of an extramarital romance. Another rumour mentioned the feathers and the four marks on the millionaire's skull. The wounds were vaguely reminiscent of claw marks made by a giant bird, and since chickens and feathers were used in ritual sacrifices, there was speculation that Sir Harry's murder was linked to voodoo.

Ultimately, neither rumour was given much credence, but there was also talk of a mysterious yacht that had been seen near Nassau on the night of Harry's death. In time, this yacht would loom large in explanations about the murder.

As the rumours spread, the Governor General continued to contemplate his options. After several telephone conversations with Harold Christie and Erskine-Lindop, Edward decided that he would remove the Nassau police from the case. Erskine-Lindop was told to have his men stand guard, but to take no other action. The Governor General was calling in Miami investigators.

Edward vividly recalled the trip he and Wallis had made to Miami in December 1940, and the members of the Miami police force who had served as his bodyguard. Now he put in a call to the chief of police and requested two officers by name: Captain Edward Melchen and Captain James Barker. Reluctant to provide too many details over the telephone, the duke said he needed them to investigate the death, "under extraordinary circumstances," of a prominent citizen. He provided no further details, but made it clear that the matter was urgent. He arranged for Pan American Airlines to delay its noon flight until the police officers were aboard.

* * *

Around the time Edward completed arrangements with the Miami police, Freddie de Marigny returned to Nassau. He had spent most of the morning on his rural chicken farm, working alongside his foreman George Thompson and others. The first person he encountered on his return to town was John H. Anderson, manager of the Bahamas General Trust Company. When Anderson broke the news of Sir Harry's death, Freddie was astounded. "Are you kidding?" he asked. Together, the two men drove out to Westbourne, but rather than go to the Oakes mansion, they stopped at the Kelly cottage. While Anderson talked to Madeline Kelly, who had returned to her house by this time, Freddie walked towards Westbourne. He returned 15 minutes later, claiming he felt ill.

A short time later, Freddie returned to Westbourne. A number of policemen were in the house, including Commissioner Erskine-Lindop. Unable to investigate, they were relegated to guarding the murder scene and keeping visitors under control. As soon as word of Sir Harry's death got around, friends and curiosity-seekers from all over Nassau converged on the house. There was little attempt to keep them out.

Thousands of kilometres away, Lady Eunice received

the news by telegram. When she called Westbourne to confirm the details of the tragedy, Harold Christie answered the
phone. Freddie asked to speak to his mother-in-law, but
Christie ignored him and began to hang up. Freddie took
the receiver from Christie and spoke to Lady Eunice, offer-
ing his sympathies and reminding her to inform Nancy. He
also asked Lady Eunice to have Nancy call him as soon as
she could.

After hanging up the phone, Freddie turned on Harold
Christie. Why had he not informed him of his father-in-law's
death? They were friends — in fact, Freddie had invited
Christie to a dinner party the night before. Christie stuttered
an excuse and went to talk to the attorney general. Freddie
then spoke to Erskine-Lindop, who told him that Miami
detectives were on the way. He seemed embarrassed that his
men could do nothing but wait for outsiders to arrive.

After Sir Harry's body was placed in an ambu-
lance for transportation to the General Hospital, Freddie
left Westbourne. Eventually so did Attorney General Eric
Hallinan, who met the Miami detectives at the airport shortly
before 2 p.m.

Captain Edward Melchen was 50. He had served as a
clerk in various departments before becoming Miami's chief
of homicide and, since 1933, he had also been assigned as
a bodyguard to visiting celebrities. Accompanying him was
Captain James O. Barker. Ten years younger than Melchen,
Barker had been a motorcycle cop and a clerk in the Bureau

of Criminal Identification, but had been demoted because of insubordination. He had, however, returned to the bureau, become its superintendent, and was considered an expert on fingerprints.

People were already asking questions about the Miami detectives. Why had they been brought in? The answer lay with the Duke of Windsor. He did not have confidence in the Bahamian police. There was no question of sending to Britain for official assistance, not only because of the greater distance, but also because it was wartime and resources were severely limited. Miami was certainly closer, and he was already acquainted with police officers there.

Once again, the former king's actions reflected his lack of judgment. The Miami police department was reputed to be one of the most corrupt in the United States. Nevertheless, Bahamian officials were determined to present the Governor General's decision in the most positive light. Attorney General Eric Hallinan told reporters that the Miami police-men had brought with them the most up-to-date fingerprint equipment. The truth was something altogether different. Although Hallinan may not have been aware of it at the time, Barker had forgotten to bring a fingerprint camera, the most important piece of equipment at his disposal. To save face, the policemen announced that it was too humid to dust for prints, so they would have to wait for morning. Meanwhile, someone put out word that, when the Miami police were first contacted, they were led to believe that the death had been a suicide. In fact, by this time Sir Harry's body had already been examined and the possibility of suicide eliminated.

Freddie de Marigny would later claim there was something fishy about the investigation right from the start. A few hours after Sir Harry's body was taken away for autopsy, Freddie called his friend Dr. Ulrich Oberwarth. Oberwarth had conducted the post-mortem, but refused to discuss the matter over the telephone. Instead, he offered to drop by Freddie's house later that afternoon. When Oberwarth arrived, he revealed that he had been instructed not to write down the details of what he found.

By this time, Melchen and Barker had reached Westbourne, where they began asking questions about Sir Harry: his habits, his business interests, his friends, and most importantly, his enemies. Around seven o'clock that evening, they learned from Erskine-Lindop about the stormy relationship between Sir Harry and his son-in-law. At that point, the police commissioner sent one of his police officers, Lieutenant John Douglas, to bring Freddie to Westbourne.

By this time, the Miami detectives were convinced that whoever had killed Sir Harry had deliberately set the bed on fire, hoping that the house would burn and hide evidence of the crime. Although the storm had ruined those plans, the police reasoned, the guilty party would probably have some evidence of the blaze on his body.

They narrowed their suspects to three men. One was Harold Christie. Christie said he had been in the house all night. Although Sir Harry's room was 6 metres (20 feet) away, Christie claimed he had heard nothing going on in Sir Harry's room, even though he had been awakened by mosquitoes and thunder during the night.

His presence at Westbourne on the night in question was not the only reason Harold Christie came under police scrutiny. Christie was spending money almost as fast as he could earn it, pouring a fortune into the tourist resort he was developing at Lyford Cay, on one end of New Providence Island. There was talk, too, that he wanted to bring casinos to the Bahamas. Even though gambling was illegal, plenty of people were convinced that if Christie could persuade Harry Oakes to support the idea of casinos, the laws could be changed.

When they found no burns or singed hairs on Christie's body, the detectives turned to their second suspect—Harcourt Maura. Maura was Sir Harry's stable master, and it was common knowledge that the two men had recently quarrelled. Again the detectives found nothing to arouse suspicion.

The third suspect was Freddie de Marigny. Melchen examined Freddie carefully, looking at his beard, arms, chest, hair, fingers, and fingernails. Although there was no blood or human tissue under Freddie's fingernails, there were burned hairs on his hand and arms.

Freddie explained that he had been working at his chicken farm that morning, preparing chickens for market. Although a machine removed most of the feathers from the birds, a certain amount of fluffy down remained. The most efficient way to remove it was to hold the birds over a flame. Burns to the hands and arms were commonplace. In addition, Freddie said, he had burned his hand the night before, when the storm had hit during a dinner party at his house, knocking out the electric lights. Freddie had lighted two hurricane lamps by inserting his hand through the tops of the glass shades, burning it in the process.

Naturally, the police questioned his whereabouts. Freddie revealed that he had driven two of his female guests home about 1 a.m. and was home and in bed by 1:15. His cousin Georges could vouch for him. However, the police wanted more, and asked him to produce the clothes he wore that night. If Freddie was their man, they reasoned, there would be blood or other evidence on his clothing.

Melchen, Barker, and Erskine-Lindop went home with Freddie. When Melchen asked him to find the tie and shirt he had worn the previous night, Freddie could not comply. He owned at least 30 ties, he explained, and was not sure which one he had been wearing. As for the shirt, all of them were either white or cream, and Freddie was uncertain which one he had worn.

"Do you refuse to show me the shirt you wore last night?" Melchen asked.

Freddie thought he was joking and suggested the maid might have the answer. Since she was gone for the day, Melchen might try looking through the laundry basket.

Freddie did remember that he had been wearing a light brown jacket with darker brown pants the previous evening. As Melchen hunted for the shirt and tie, Barker had gone through Freddie's closet and located the suit. He was not happy with what he found. "This suit is freshly pressed," he said to Freddie. "How do you account for that?"

Freddie was losing his temper. The questions seemed stupid to him. At that point, Erskine-Lindop came into the room and asked if anything was wrong. Barker held out the suit and repeated, "It is freshly pressed."

Freddie had had enough. "The laundress does it every day," he explained, then asked Erskine-Lindop to confirm.

The police commissioner did just that. It was customary in the islands at a time when labour was cheap and permanent press fabrics did not exist. "It gives one a good presence," Erskine-Lindop explained, "and is a very British tradition."

The police were dubious and far from satisfied with the results of their investigation when they left for the night. Before they left, however, they assigned Lieutenant John Douglas to stay with Freddie. Every half-hour or so until morning, one of them called Douglas to make sure everything was still in order.

Sometime during their long night together, Freddie asked Douglas if a man could be convicted by circumstantial evidence if the murder weapon could not be found. The question may have been prompted by little more than curiosity about the legal process, but when Douglas repeated it, it took on a sinister character.

Freddie agreed to return to Westbourne the following morning. He drove his own car, with Douglas sitting
beside him in the passenger seat. Arriving shortly before the
appointed time, they found that several other people had
already gathered at the Oakes mansion, including Freddie's
cousin Georges de Visdelou, Effie Henneage, who had been
among the guests at Westbourne on the night of the murder,
and Jean Ainsley and Dorothy Clark, the women Freddie had
driven home from his own dinner party.

One by one, the various individuals were asked to step
into a downstairs study for questioning. When Freddie's turn
came, he was told to follow Melchen upstairs. They sat facing
one another on wicker chairs in a small room with a view of
the ocean. Between them was a glass-topped table on which
sat a carafe of water and two clean glasses.

Melchen asked a number of questions. Who might have
a grudge against Sir Harry? What did Freddie know about
Harold Christie? As Freddie responded, the Miami detective
pulled out a packet of cigarettes still wrapped in cellophane
and tossed it onto the table. "Have one," he offered.

Freddie accepted, with thanks. He lit a cigarette for
himself, then replaced the package on the table. Melchen did
not touch it. More questions followed, focussing on Freddie's
stormy relationship with Sir Harry. At one point, Melchen
told Freddie someone had seen him at Westbourne on the
night of the murder.

Freddie challenged him to produce a witness.

Melchen nodded, seemingly unconcerned. A moment or two later, he asked Freddie to pour him a glass of water and take one himself. Freddie complied, and as he handed one to Melchen, James Barker poked his head into the room. "Everything all right?" he asked his partner. Melchen assured him that it was, as he stood up and escorted Freddie downstairs. They now had Freddie's fingerprints.

Freddie spent the rest of the day taking care of various items of business. Meanwhile, the Duke of Windsor paid a call to Westbourne and spent about 20 minutes in conversation with James Barker. Soon after he left, word spread that an arrest was imminent.

Between 5 and 6 p.m., Freddie was having cocktails with friends at the St. George Hotel, when Lieutenant John Douglas arrived. Douglas announced that Freddie was wanted at Westbourne. Freddie protested that he was about to have dinner. Douglas insisted, and the two men drove back out to the estate.

Again, Melchen questioned him about visiting Westbourne on the night in question. Again, Freddie denied it. He was escorted into the living room, where Colonel Erskine-Lindop and Attorney General Eric Hallinan were waiting. Hallinan beckoned him closer. "Alfred de Marigny," he said, "you are accused of the murder of Sir Harry Oakes. Have you anything to say?"

"I do not know what you want me to say," Freddie

replied. He was increasingly confused, especially when Melchen warned him that nobody was "too small or too big to be arrested."

Freddie was still protesting the ridiculousness of the accusation when Hallinan motioned to Erksine-Lindop. The commissioner of police stepped forward and placed his right hand on Freddie's shoulder, while announcing, "Alfred de Marigny, in the name of the Crown, you are under arrest for the murder of Sir Harry Oakes."

Freddie was cautioned. He was advised that he did not have to make a statement, but that any statement he might make would be admissible in court. Then he was asked if he wanted to call an attorney.

Alfred Adderley was the first man who came to mind. The barrister who had been succeeded by Harry Oakes in the Legislative Assembly was the best criminal lawyer in the Bahamas. Whether representing the accused or the Crown, he had never lost a murder case. Hallinan went to a phone and called, but could not reach Adderley. He told Freddie a message would be sent.

Lieutenant John Douglas and two other policemen escorted Freddie to the Court of Justice. Asked by Magistrate F. E. Fields if he wanted an attorney present, Freddie explained that a message had been left for Alfred Adderley. Fields cleared his throat and told him that Adderley had been hired as part of the Crown's prosecution team.

Shaken, unable to think clearly, and not trusting

himself to speak, Freddie heard Fields say that the court would appoint a lawyer for him. But the attorney who arrived was Stafford Sands, a corporate lawyer. As Freddie saw his chances of a competent defense fading, Sands explained his presence was merely a formality. Godfrey Higgs would be back in Nassau after the weekend and would then take over the case.

At a brief hearing, Freddie provided a voluntary statement. "It is a ridiculous charge, as I have no reason to do it," he insisted after being charged with the murder. He described his activities on the night Sir Harry was killed and the morning the body was discovered. "I can say, swear, that I have not seen Sir Harry Oakes to talk to since the 29th of March." After noting that he had not been to Westbourne since a short visit two years previously, Freddie concluded, "This is all I have to say."

Freddie's protest of innocence was duly recorded before he was escorted to a cell in the Nassau jail.

Chapter 5
Preliminaries

The Nassau jail had been built more than a century earlier. It was a formidable stone fortress, accessible by an iron gate just wide enough to allow one car to enter. Everything about it was designed to intimidate those hapless individuals imprisoned there.

Freddie's cell had whitewashed walls and a stone floor. On one side was a barred window set so high in the wall that even Freddie, at 6 feet, 5 inches, could not look out. The stone floor was host to a collection of vermin, including rats, spiders, and other insects. Along one wall was a small wooden stool with a washbasin and water pitcher. A covered bucket served as a toilet. There was

Murder!

Police escorting de Marigny to a preliminary court hearing

nowhere to sit except for a narrow folding cot, which was too short to provide much comfort for a tall man.

Alfred de Marigny may not have been the wealthiest or most powerful individual in Nassau prior to his arrest, but imprisonment immediately made it clear just how privileged his life had been up to that moment. The turnkey apologized as he locked Freddie in his cell. He could not bring him a pillow or blanket that night because it was after hours and the storeroom was closed. Nor could he turn off the two electric lights that burned brightly from the domed ceiling of the cell. Under orders from the attorney general, the lights were to be left on at all times. Eric Hallinan was taking no chances that Freddie might escape or attempt suicide.

Hallinan's power also extended to Freddie's personal appearance. While Nancy was away in the United States, Freddie had decided to surprise her by growing a beard and moustache. Now he wanted to shave it, for two important reasons. First, given the primitive sanitation in the jail, it would be easier for Freddie to keep clean if he shaved off his beard. Second, he was aware that many people were prejudiced against beards. They seemed sinister, somehow less respectable, calling to mind revolutionaries, pirates, and fugitives who wanted to hide their identities behind whiskers. Unfortunately for Freddie, the attorney general was also aware of this popular prejudice. At his insistence, the beard remained.

While Freddie marked time in jail, preparations were made to transport his father-in-law's remains back to the United States. On Sunday, July 11, the body of Sir Harry Oakes was flown out of Nassau. Before the plane reached Miami, however, the pilot was instructed to turn back. Sir Harry's body was returned to the morgue at Nassau General Hospital, where photographs were taken of his fingerprints. The following day, his body was again prepared for transport. This time a British military plane carried him to Miami, where the body was shipped by train to Dover-Foxcroft, Harry's childhood home near Bar Harbor.

Freddie's arraignment took place on Monday. The Crown presented a formidable team in Attorney General Eric Hallinan and barrister Alfred Adderley. Godfrey Higgs, the defense lawyer, was certainly a match for Adderley — the two had locked horns on several occasions. However, Higgs's young associate, Ernest Callender, was far less experienced than the prosecution. Before the trial had even begun, it was clear that Freddie was at a disadvantage.

As he walked into the courthouse that morning, Freddie passed Alfred Adderley, the man he had originally wanted to defend him. He did not mince words. "At least you could have had the courtesy of sending me a refusal," he told Adderley.

"I don't know what you mean," the barrister responded.

"You did not have the courtesy even to acknowledge my request before turning me down."

Adderley was astonished when he learned that Freddie had wanted to retain him. "Had I received such a request," he explained, "professional ethics would have demanded that I see you in person. I assure you, this is the first I have heard of such a request." Someone, it seemed, had deliberately prevented the message from reaching Adderley.

The arraignment was brief. At the request of the Crown, proceedings were adjourned for a week to allow for further investigation.

Meanwhile, Sir Harry was laid to rest in Dover-Foxcroft.

The funeral was scheduled for July 15, with an old friend of Sir Harry officiating. Melchen and Barker attended the service, then called on Lady Oakes in her Bar Harbor home that afternoon. Prostrate with grief, she was in bed, still trying to cope with the shock of her husband's murder.

The information the policemen relayed brought little comfort. As Nancy Oakes de Marigny would later testify, they revealed graphic details about Sir Harry's last moments. The murderer had apparently taken a wooden balustrade from a pile located beneath the second-floor veranda at Westbourne. He then climbed the stairs, slipped into Sir Harry's room, and clubbed him on the head. Then, the murderer had sprayed the bed with an oil-based insecticide and set it on fire.

Stunned but still alive, Sir Harry had felt the heat of the flames and tried to rise from the bed. He fought with his assailant, and, during the struggle, an ornate, six-panel Chinese screen had been knocked over. The murderer stood it up, moving it to block a window so the flames could not be seen by anyone outside.

Realizing her mother was close to hysterics, Nancy ordered the two policemen out of the room. Once Lady Eunice was somewhat calmer, Nancy rejoined them and they continued their story. The fire and the beating had finally killed Sir Harry, Barker told her. But the Chinese screen had a tale to tell. A careful examination had revealed a fingerprint — one that belonged to her husband, Alfred de Marigny.

Nancy refused to believe that Freddie was responsible

for her father's death and said as much. But Barker was adamant. They had caught the killer, and it was only a matter of time before he was convicted.

Two days later, just before boarding a Pan Am clipper for Nassau, Captain Melchen spoke to the press. He told them that Sir Harry had been bludgeoned, then sprayed with a flammable liquid. He had lived for about five minutes longer, during which time the attacker had set fire to the bed. The fire had likely been set to cover the traces of the murder, which might have succeeded if the heavy rains had not doused the blaze.

On July 18, Nancy left New York's LaGuardia Airport on her way to Miami, and then to Nassau. She told reporters that she "had formed no opinion" concerning Freddie's involvement with her father's death. As soon as she could, she visited Freddie in jail. Although the meeting was awkward because an official had to be present at all times, the couple was able to discuss the details of the murder, Freddie's arrest, and the various accusations levelled at him. On July 21, when more reporters interviewed Nancy at the de Marigny cottage, she announced that she had made up her mind. "I am firmly convinced that Freddie did not commit this crime," she said. "The course of human nature is unpredictable, but from my knowledge of him, such a possibility is absolutely fantastic."

By this time, Nancy had hired Raymond C. Schindler, a flamboyant private detective who had solved several sensational cases. Freddie was not particularly happy with the arrangement, since Schindler's fee was $300 a day plus expenses, and they needed every cent they could scrape together to pay Freddie's legal fees. Freddie had sold all his property and his beloved boat, while Nancy had cashed in some bonds and shares in her father's mine. But Nancy was insistent about hiring the detective. Not only was Schindler famous for his investigative techniques, he also had an excellent relationship with the press. At 19, Nancy instinctively understood how important good public relations could be to Freddie's case.

Raymond Schindler was around 60, a large, heavyset man who enjoyed the good life. Like Freddie de Marigny, he loved good food, amusing company, and pretty women. He also had something in common with Harry Oakes. After starting out as an insurance agent, Schindler had gone west in search of gold. He found none, but he did stumble into a career as a private investigator. He later opened his own company, where he built a reputation on solid, painstaking research and creative detective work.

When Nancy approached him, Schindler agreed to take the case on one condition: if he turned up information that indicated Freddie's guilt, he would resign and turn over his findings to the police. Completely convinced of Freddie's innocence, Nancy agreed.

Soon after Schindler arrived in Nassau, Godfrey Higgs arranged for him to visit Westbourne, but when Schindler arrived, he was horrified to find Nassau policemen wiping the walls of the landing outside Sir Harry's room. Schindler demanded to know why they were removing bloody hand-prints and any remaining fingerprints. The policemen replied that they were just following orders. Then they added. "They're not those of the accused person. They will only con-fuse the evidence."

The situation inside Sir Harry's room was not much better. Melchen and Barker had dusted all the prints, and, after several days of humid July weather, the prints were completely useless.

Schindler quickly recognized that he would get little help from the Nassau police, or from Melchen and Barker. He also realized that he was being watched and that his tele-phone was tapped. To flush out the eavesdroppers, he picked a name at random from the telephone directory and dialed the number. Without introducing himself, he told the person answering the phone to meet him at a specific time at Fort Charlotte, an eighteenth-century fortress that was a local landmark. He repeated the process twice more. At the agreed time, he surreptitiously caught a cab and told the driver to go to the Fort. When he arrived, two police cars were waiting.

Schindler was convinced that someone was going to great lengths to prevent him from turning up evidence that might help Freddie. That alone suggested that someone else was responsible for Sir Harry's death. But Schindler had built his reputation on leaving no stone unturned. He continued his investigation behind the scenes, assisted by Leonard

Keeler, a fingerprint expert and head of the first police crime laboratory in the United States. All the while, Schindler continued feeding positive information about Freddie to the press. He also put the defense team in contact with a number of forensic experts.

* * *

Freddie's preliminary hearing opened on July 21. Dr. Hugh A. Quackenbush described what he had seen in the master bedroom at Westbourne, including the burns on the carpet and on the outside of a wardrobe. Then Dr. L. W. Fitzmaurice, chief medical officer of the Bahamas General Hospital, testified about the autopsy findings. Sir Harry had died of shock, brain hemorrhage, and a fractured skull. The murder weapon, which was yet to be found, was "a hard, blunt instrument having a well-defined edge."

Following medical testimony, the preliminary hearing was abruptly postponed for another week. In the interim, Major Herbert Pemberton, chief of the Criminal Investigation Department of the Nassau Bahamas police force, headed to New York in the company of Captain Melchen. Their mission was to discuss "very important" new evidence with experts. Although the details were not revealed at the time, that evidence was apparently the fingerprints Barker had discussed with Lady Oakes on the day of the funeral. Pemberton and Melchen brought with them copies of Freddie's fingerprints, and spent several hours examining fingerprint files at the New York City Police College.

On July 26, the preliminary hearing reopened. Dorothy Turley Clark and Jean Ainsley testified. Both were married to RAF officers and lived in adjoining cottages. They had attended Freddie's dinner party the night of the murder, and testified that he drove them home around 1:30 a.m. The route he travelled brought him close to Westbourne.

When Magistrate Fields announced that the hearing would be adjourned for another week, Godfrey Higgs strenuously objected. He had heard from the detectives that the investigation would be drawn out until October, which, he argued, contravened Freddie's right to a speedy trial. He had also heard rumours that "surprise evidence" would be revealed at the last moment. Alfred Adderley assured Higgs that Freddie would not be victimized, but added that the delays were not unusual in a murder case. Magistrate Fields conceded that Adderley was right, but still instructed the prosecution to speed up matters as much as possible.

Meanwhile, Freddie was confined to jail. Nancy saw him when she could, but their visits were still closely supervised. She also arranged for his meals to be brought from home, a practice followed by the families of most prisoners. For Freddie, it was one small comfort in an otherwise bleak existence.

To keep in shape, he exercised in his cell, running in place and doing push-ups. He mulled over recent events, trying to recall every shred of information that might help his lawyers. Sometimes, the only things that kept him from plunging into despair were the sound of music from a nearby nightclub and the words of encouragement offered by Captain R. M. Miller, superintendent of the Nassau jail. The morning after he was imprisoned, Freddie was called to Miller's office. Over coffee and toast, Miller asked several questions, including whether or not Freddie had killed Sir Harry. Freddie swore he had nothing to do with the murder.

According to Freddie, Miller said he believed in his innocence, but that as soon as he had heard of Sir Harry's murder, he knew Freddie would be arrested for the crime. He could do very little to make Freddie's stay in jail more comfortable, but he did offer some sound advice: "Conduct yourself not only as a man, but as an *innocent* man. Be dignified. Be calm. Give yourself the best chance you can. Never forget they are out to hang you."

The hearing ran for three days during the first week of August. On Thursday, August 5, Frank Conway, a detective with the New York City Criminal Identification Department, discussed fingerprints. Conway had been consulted in New York by the Miami detectives and was considered an expert in the field. According to him, a fingerprint found on the Chinese screen in Sir Harry's room belonged to Freddie. As the court was shown photos of the fingerprint, Freddie smiled and stroked his beard. He was determined to appear as unperturbed as possible.

There was no court stenographer to take down the proceedings, no stenography machine to make the job easier.
Magistrate Fields copied notes in longhand. By Thursday,
after three days of writing, his fingers were sore. He adjourned
the hearing until the following Tuesday, August 10.

Harold Christie was the most important witness called
on when the hearing resumed. Christie told how he had
found the body of the man he described as his best friend.
Then he spoke of conversations with Freddie, including a
recent one in which Freddie complained about Sir Harry's
refusal to sell him a certain piece of land. Christie repeated
stories about the friction between Sir Harry and Freddie.
According to Christie, Freddie had told him that Sir Harry
was particularly irked by Freddie's bad treatment of Ruth, his
former wife. Freddie was annoyed with Sir Harry because he
refused to listen to his version of events.

The hearing dragged on, interspersed with many
adjournments. On August 23, Lady Eunice reached the island
in the company of her lawyer. Returning to Westbourne was
too painful for her, so she stayed with Sir Harry's Nassau lawyer, Kenneth Solomon. Soon after her arrival, word spread
that she would testify at the preliminary hearing.

Before Lady Oakes took the stand, however, police
Lieutenant John Douglas recounted the time he had spent
guarding Freddie, from late afternoon of July 8 until his arrest
on July 9. At one point, Douglas recalled, Freddie had blurted

out, "That guy should have been killed anyhow!"

Lady Oakes appeared pale and fragile as she took the stand. She was wearing deep mourning, a constant reminder of her dreadful loss, and as she spoke, she frequently sobbed. Much of her testimony centred on the feud between Harry and Freddie, including the fact that she and Harry had changed their wills in February after learning of Nancy's pregnancy. Under the new wills, until she was 30, Nancy would receive only an allowance, rather than a share of the entire Oakes estate. When Lady Oakes finished her testimony, she was so emotionally drained that Nancy had to help her from the stand.

The final bit of testimony that day came from John Anderson, the bank manager who had told Freddie about the murder and driven him to the Newell Kelly cottage. Anderson provided details of Freddie's financial situation. He revealed that Freddie was short of cash and wanted to borrow $125,000 to avoid being sued by his former wife.

On Monday, August 31, Magistrate Fields made his ruling. "I am satisfied that a prima facie case has been made out against you," he told the accused, "and I order you to stand trial at court in the October sessions."

Freddie's face was expressionless as he heard the news. Nancy, also, seemed very controlled, although some reporters sensed tension in her posture. It had been more than seven weeks since her father's murder. Now, she and Freddie faced the prospect of another seven-week wait before the trial began.

In the interim, both sides prepared their case. At one time, before the trial began on October 18, policemen visited the de Marigny residence. Nancy, who was home alone at the time, claimed she had asked for a warrant, but Deputy Commissioner Pemberton refused to produce one. When she asked to call a lawyer, the police ignored her request. They searched the house, then left. She did not know whether they had taken anything with them.

Freddie spent the time before his trial conferring with his lawyer, talking to Nancy when she visited, and directing the operation of his chicken farm from his cell.

On October 2, Lady Oakes arrived in Nassau along with her lawyer and Newell Kelly. Three days later, Sir Harry's will was filed for probate, which made the contents a matter of public record. Soon, the newspapers were carrying the details. Sir Harry's personal estate was estimated at $14,636,000. One-third had been bequeathed to Eunice. The remainder was to be split among the five children, making Nancy's inheritance just under $2 million. Contrary to rumours circulating since the murder, she had not been disinherited. Although she would have to live on an annual allowance of about £2,500 until she was 30, Nancy Oakes de Marigny was a very rich woman. Her inheritance was more than enough to provide a solid motive for murder.

On the day the will was filed for probate, the attorney general finally gave Freddie permission to shave his moustache and beard.

Chapter 6
The Trial Begins

The trial opened on October 18 at the Nassau courthouse. The courtroom was a small, old chamber, decorated with wooden panelling. The bench, at the centre front, dominated the room. On the judge's left was the jurors' box. On his right was the prisoner's pen, essentially a cage — a box-like structure with bars at the front and a lid that closed down upon the accused. Arranged before the bench were two curved tables, one for the prosecution, one for the defense. Behind these was a wooden railing with a gate, which separated onlookers from the court. The front row of seating was reserved for reporters; the remaining rows were available for spectators. Wealthy Bahamians who wanted to watch the spectacle sent their servants to the court early in the morning to save a seat for them. Officially, there was room for 105, but because the case had drawn so much attention, many more crammed into the room to watch from makeshift seating.

Freddie, clean-shaven and calm, took his seat in the prisoner's box and folded his arms across his chest. He did not smile. He had lost weight during his three months in jail and was suffering from the flu. Furthermore, Nancy, who had been so supportive in the weeks leading up to the trial, was on the list of witnesses scheduled to testify. For that reason, she would not be allowed in the courtroom during the proceedings, and Freddie would not be able to take comfort from her presence.

Alfred Adderley summarized the case in his opening statement, emphasizing the motive for the murder of Sir Harry Oakes. De Marigny, he stated, had killed Sir Harry for three reasons: revenge, satisfaction, and gain. Freddie had resented the way Sir Harry and Lady Eunice had treated him. During the first year of marriage, he had "enjoyed" £3,500 of Sir Harry's money — presumably the $10,000 honeymoon gift from Eunice. While Nancy's parents had tried to make the best of a bad situation, the aborted pregnancy had marked the turning point. Harry and Eunice had changed their wills, effectively ensuring that Freddie would not profit from his marriage to their daughter.

Adderley also pointed out the timing of the murder. This, he argued, was not mere coincidence. Sir Harry had been about to leave the Bahamas, and Nancy was already in the United States. If Freddie was worried that his father-in-law would exert more influence on Nancy while they were away from Nassau, he had to act before Sir Harry caught his plane.

Then Adderley broached the defense's anticipated arguments. He brought up the statement by Captain Edward Sears, the policeman who claimed that he had seen Harold Christie in a station wagon in Nassau around midnight, at precisely the time when Christie claimed he had been in bed at Westbourne. As far as Adderley was concerned, this would be "a question of Christie's personal honour and in no way will impeach the evidence of the Crown against the accused."

Finally, the prosecution turned to the fingerprint — the key piece of evidence in the Crown's case. "The fingerprint is proof that the accused was in the murdered man's house the night of the crime," he insisted. He also pointed to other evidence that implicated Freddie — his "desperate" financial situation, his inability to produce the shirt he had worn on the night of the murder, and his burned hand and singed hairs.

When Adderley finished, the jury was taken to Westbourne to familiarize themselves with the scene of the crime. Freddie was there as well. Although the jurors were under strict orders not to speak to him, most of them glanced uncomfortably in his direction as they were guided through the rooms where Sir Harry had lived and died.

Mabel Ellis, Sir Harry's housekeeper, was the first witness to take the stand the next morning. She answered seemingly routine questions, telling how Harold Christie had stayed at Westbourne on the night of Tuesday, July 6, and how he and Sir Harry had driven to town together the next morning. They had used Christie's station wagon, which was parked, as usual, at the entrance to Westbourne. Mabel also told how she had prepared Sir Harry's bedroom on the Wednesday night, laying out his pyjamas, arranging the mosquito netting, spraying the room with insecticide, then setting out an electric fan at the foot of the bed. The fan was not plugged in.

Harold Christie was the next witness. His testimony was crucial, not only because he had found Sir Harry's body, but because he was a close friend and business associate. As the questioning proceeded, it became apparent that Christie was under enormous strain.

The courtroom was not particularly warm, as it was October and the worst of the summer heat had dissipated. Yet, as he stood in the witness box, Harold Christie sweated profusely, perspiration staining the armpits and back of his white linen suit. Periodically he wiped the sweat from his face with a white handkerchief, which quickly became sodden.

His obvious anxiety was a dramatic change from his usual relaxed behaviour. There was nothing casual about his behaviour in the witness box. When Hallinan questioned him about his stay at Westbourne, he rambled on about the Oakes family being away. At times, he clutched the railing in front of him so hard that his knuckles turned white.

Point by point, Hallinan drew information from him about his activities in the hours before the murder and his relationship with Freddie de Marigny. At times, Christie seemed more relaxed. He was calm as he described the last afternoon of Sir Harry's life: they had met at the Royal Victoria Hotel, picked up Sir Harry's exit permit, and driven to Christie's house to get a tennis racket and tennis shoes. Then, after relaxing for an hour at Westbourne, they had played tennis with Christie's niece and one of her friends, until Charles Hubbard and Effie Henneage arrived. After the girls left, the foursome had dined together at Westbourne. Around 11, Sir Harry offered to drive Mrs. Henneage home, but when Hubbard insisted on doing so, Sir Harry and Christie had walked them to Hubbard's car.

When Hallinan asked about Christie's own vehicle, Christie began to sweat again. He had left the station wagon downtown after meeting Sir Harry at noon on Wednesday. At nine that evening, his driver had called Westbourne and Christie had told him to drive the car to the country club and leave it there. He did not see the station wagon again until the next morning.

At great length, Christie recounted the events of the following morning and his discovery of Sir Harry's body. Again, he seemed very tense, but most observers probably assumed this was normal, considering the horrific scene he described. He told how he had tried to revive Sir Harry, how he had shouted for help, how he had called Madeline Kelly, his brother Frank, and Police Commissioner Erskine-Lindop. He did not, however, mention his phone conversations with the Duke of Windsor.

Nor did Godfrey Higgs probe that particular matter during his cross-examination. Members of the royal family were still treated with deference in 1943. Despite his personal interest in the case and his friendship with both Sir Harry and Harold Christie, the Duke of Windsor was not asked to make an official statement and he and Wallis were conveniently away from the Bahamas during the trial.

Higgs began slowly, inoffensively. Like Christie, he was in his mid-40s. But unlike the paunchy, balding, real estate dealer, Higgs was slim and athletic-looking with carefully combed, fine black hair and light eyes that contrasted sharply with his tanned face. Compared to Adderley, who was well known for his eloquent oratory, Higgs was plainspoken, relying more on logic and careful tactics to ferret out the truth.

One bit of truth that he forced out of Christie was that relations between Freddie and Sir Harry were not as horrible as everyone had suggested. Christie, who knew Sir Harry's business dealings intimately, revealed that the millionaire had offered his son-in-law a large tract of property — more than 405 hectares (1,000 acres) — to develop. He was also considering making Freddie manager of a trust company he was about to purchase.

Higgs could not change Christie's story about Freddie's dinner invitation, however. Freddie had stated at the preliminary hearing that Christie had turned down his invitation, saying that he would be staying at Westbourne that night. Christie denied it, saying he did not have any plans to stay at Westbourne until eight that evening, long after Freddie had spoken to him. Higgs made it clear that he did not believe him, but Christie was adamant.

The main part of Higgs's cross-examination focussed on two important issues: the whereabouts of Christie's car on the night of the murder and Christie's actions after discovering the body.

Christie had left his car downtown after meeting Sir Harry, but about nine o'clock on Wednesday evening, he had received a telephone call from one of his servants, a man named Gibson. On Christie's instructions, Gibson had left the station wagon near the tennis court and hidden the keys. He wanted the car close by, Christie told Higgs, because he would be going out the next day. But he did not want the vehicle too close to the house. "I wanted to conserve my gasoline, and if it had been brought over to Westbourne, there was a good chance of my car being used," he testified. Christie was sweating heavily again as Higgs probed further, pointing out that Sir Harry had two cars at Westbourne and Charles Hubbard's car was also there. Christie stuck to his story.

Then Higgs asked about the statement Christie had made to the police shortly after the murder, in which he said that the tennis court was the logical place to leave the car. "Why was it logical?" Higgs asked.

"It was the logical place to leave it because there was a watchman there, and none at Westbourne," Christie replied.

On the surface, Christie's explanation seemed to make sense. But the crime rate was so low on the island that Christie's car would have been safe wherever it was parked. And, with so many people dabbling in the black market, gas rationing was nothing but a minor inconvenience to someone with Christie's connections. His answers and his obvious distress on the stand indicated that he was either lying or hiding part of the truth.

Higgs then referred to a statement made by Charles Hubbard. After driving Effie Henneage home, Hubbard's route to his own place took him directly past Westbourne. In his statement, Hubbard said he saw the mansion "well lighted up." According to Christie, the lights had all been turned out, except perhaps for a small light on one porch. The light in the guest room would have been on as well, but that was all.

The discrepancy between the two statements led Higgs to question Christie's whereabouts on the night of the murder. "Did you leave Westbourne *any* time that night?" he asked.

"I did not leave Westbourne any time during the night of July 7, or until the next night of July 8." Christie's statement was unequivocal, but his body language told another tale. He was gripping the rail of the witness box so tightly that his knuckles were white. He also blinked nervously and rolled his head about, as though to relieve tension in his neck and shoulders.

That tension increased as Higgs turned to a statement made by Nassau's superintendent of police. Captain Edward De Witt Sears was a close friend of Christie's brother, Frank. All three had attended the local grammar school around the same time. On the night of the murder, Sears left the central police station shortly before midnight. As he drove through downtown, he passed a station wagon driving in the opposite direction. It was raining, but there was no doubt in Sears's mind that Harold Christie was sitting in the front passenger seat and that someone else was driving.

Adderley had already referred to the captain's statement in his opening remarks. Now Higgs asked more questions.

"Do you know Captain Sears, superintendent of police?"

"I do," replied Christie.

"You are friendly with him?"

"I am not friendly or unfriendly. I see very little of him."

"Have you known him since boyhood?"

"Yes."

"He has no ill-will against you that you know of?"

"No."

"If Captain Sears were to say that he had seen you in town the night of July 7th, what would you say?"

"I would say that Captain Sears is very seriously mistaken and should be more careful in his observations."

Higgs pushed. "I put it to you that Captain Sears saw

you at about midnight in a station wagon in George Street."

(The phrase "I put it to you" was deliberately belliger-
ent, a challenge typically issued in British courts when bar-
risters did not believe what they were being told.)

"Was he certain?" Christie retorted.

"I put it to you," Higgs repeated.

Christie denied everything. "Captain Sears was mistaken.
I did not leave Westbourne after retiring to my room that night
until the next night, and any statement to the effect that I was in
town is a very grave mistake." He conceded that Sears was a reputable person, but even reputable people could be mistaken.

Under oath, Sears would later confirm his statement.
He was positive it was Harold Christie he had seen on the
night of the murder.

By this time it was close to 5 p.m., so court was
adjourned. The next morning, Harold Christie was back
in the witness box. Once more it was only a few moments
before his white linen suit and white shirt were soaked
with perspiration.

Godfrey Higgs resumed his cross-examination by refer-
ring to the testimony of Mabel Ellis. The housekeeper claimed
that Sir Harry and Christie always dressed before breakfast.
Christie contradicted this, saying that they usually dressed
early if they were going out.

"Why did you not dress for breakfast on Thursday
morning?" Higgs asked. Christie had already stated that he
and Sir Harry were planning to go out.

Christie seemed to misunderstand. "After I discovered the body?"

"Before you discovered it. Were you going out after breakfast?"

There was a long pause, one of several that occurred during Christie's testimony. Erle Stanley Gardner, creator of the Perry Mason mystery series, was in court covering the trial for a newspaper syndicate. By his watch, it was 37 seconds before Christie responded. He bit his lip, looked around the courtroom, then avoided the question completely.

"Sir Harry rose at daybreak, and he usually could be found looking out over the water," he said.

Higgs would not let it go. "But you were planning to go out that morning?"

Christie nodded vaguely. "Yes. At 10:30."

Then the questions turned to the discovery of the body. Sir Harry was lying face up, but not completely on his back. Instead, Christie said, he was turned slightly on his right side. Christie admitted moving Sir Harry, lifting his shoulders and shaking him before pouring some water into his mouth. He was trembling with emotion as he recalled the events of that morning.

Then Higgs asked if Christie had noticed any burning spots on Sir Harry's bed. He had not. Yet, in the statement he had made earlier, Christie admitted leaving Sir Harry's room to see if the fire had spread elsewhere.

"In searching for signs of fire, I believe you went into

the adjoining room to the east, into your bathroom, and into your bedroom?" Higgs asked.

"Yes," Christie replied.

Higgs asked why, and Christie told him he was searching for sparks and to see if anybody was in there.

Higgs's next question dripped with sarcasm: "But you had been in your bedroom all night, Mr. Christie?"

"Yes!" shouted Christie, shifting his weight from one side to another.

The sparring continued. Christie described how he had wiped blood from Sir Harry's face with a wet towel. Carefully selecting a photograph from a stack on a nearby table, Higgs held it up to Christie. "Would you say that that face has been wiped?" he asked.

Christie said that it had. Higgs drew his attention to the pattern of dried blood in his next question. "That picture shows blood flowing from the ear across the face and over the nose?"

"It does," Christie replied.

The blood had run from the wounds behind Sir Harry's left ear, past his sideburn, under the left eye and then over the bridge of his nose. Unless the law of gravity had been temporarily suspended, the only way this could have happened was if Sir Harry had been lying face down on the bed. This was not the position Christie described.

"Would that suggest to you that Sir Harry had been lying face down on the bed?"

"Yes."

"But you did not find Sir Harry that way?"

Christie said he had not. Questioned directly by Sir Oscar Bedford Daly, the chief justice, he again admitted that he had moved Sir Harry's body and placed a pillow under his head. This was the position in which it was photographed. Sir Oscar was far from happy with the news that the body had been moved.

Finally, Higgs asked about bloody handprints on both sides of Christie's bedroom door. There were also prints on both sides of a door leading to a second-storey veranda. Christie conceded that they might be his handprints, but he had no memory of going through the door to the veranda.

By the time the questioning ended, Christie was near exhaustion. The whole business had been an ordeal, especially the cross-examination, and anyone listening carefully would have realized that there were a number of unexplained details in his story. Christie's nervous shuffling, the heavy perspiration, and the long pauses before answering several questions all suggested he knew more about the murder than he was saying. But Harold Christie was not on trial, and the Crown was about to present physical evidence that placed Freddie de Marigny at the scene.

Chapter 7
Exhibit J

A parade of witnesses followed Harold Christie on the stand. Constable Wendell Lamond Parker, a Nassau policeman, recalled that early on the morning of July 8 Freddie arrived at the police station. His business had nothing to do with Harry Oakes, but concerned a new truck he had purchased for his chicken farm. According to Parker, however, Freddie looked "excited and mad" and there was a "wild look" in his eyes. In cross-examination, Higgs ridiculed Parker's testimony, planting the suggestion that Parker's interpretation of Freddie's appearance was made after the news of the murder had been reported. He also undermined Parker's credibility as a reliable eyewitness by covering his eyes and having his colleague,

Ernest Callender, ask the constable what colour Higgs's eyes were. "Blue," Parker replied. In fact, they were hazel. This called into question Parker's powers of observation.

Next, Hallinan had chief medical officer L. W. Fitzmaurice estimate the time of death. Based on stomach contents, Fitzmaurice said Sir Harry probably died between 1:30 and 3:30 a.m.

The prosecution then turned to the process of establishing Freddie's whereabouts during the crucial time period. The two women he had driven home after his party testified. The time frame was close enough to persuade listeners that Freddie had been in the neighbourhood of Westbourne at the time Sir Harry died. The statement Freddie gave to police was read into the record. Then the prosecution introduced contradictory evidence. One of Freddie's neighbours, Howard Lightbourne, said that when he returned home at 12:30 a.m., July 8, there was a bright light in Freddie's bedroom. Lightbourne went to bed, then awoke at 1:45. The light was still on. He went back to sleep, and wakened again at 4. Once more, the light was on. Lightbourne could not be cross-examined, however. Because he required surgery in the United States, he had made a sworn statement before the trial began, and it was this that was read into the record.

The issue of burns was next on the prosecution's agenda. Dr. Leonard Huggins testified that he had examined Freddie six days after the murder, but had found no burned hairs or blisters. After Captain James Barker's statement about burned hairs on Freddie's hands was read, Higgs questioned the doctor. If the burns were as extensive as Barker claimed, would not Huggins have noticed? "Yes!" Huggins replied. "I would have expected to see evidence of considerable burned hair."

On its own, burned hair was insufficient evidence to prove that Freddie had gone to Westbourne at the time of the murder. He claimed he had not been in the house since 1940. If that was the case, why was his fingerprint found in Sir Harry's bedroom? Deputy Police Commissioner Herbert Pemberton testified that Freddie had been warned about going upstairs on Thursday, July 8, after the police had arrived on the scene. Nor did he see him go upstairs on Friday, July 9. The implication was that Freddie could not have left the print behind during the time when so many people were moving in and out of the house. But when Godfrey Higgs asked him, "You are not in a position to say definitely that the accused did not go upstairs at Westbourne Friday morning?" Pemberton replied that he wasn't.

And still there was the question of Harold Christie's whereabouts. Higgs asked Pemberton if Christie's bed had been slept in. Pemberton testified that the bedding was not heavily ruffled, but someone had lain on it. He noticed that the pillow had the mark of a head, but the sheets were barely disturbed.

Before he was finished with Pemberton, Higgs turned to the fingerprints. "Did you not notice a bloody print on the inside south door of the room Christie occupied the night of the murder?"

"I did," Pemberton replied.

"Fingerprints left in blood are visible, aren't they, major?"

"Correct."

"You don't powder such prints to make them visible, do you?"

"I cannot answer that. I have never dealt with bloody fingerprints."

"Do you agree that powdering would blur a wet imprint?"

"Yes."

"Would it not have the same effect on a bloody print?"

"I am unable to say."

"Had the bloody print on the south door of Mr. Christie's room been powdered?"

"Yes."

"Didn't the powdering obscure the print?"

"I am unable to say."

Harold Christie had already testified that he might have gone to his room after discovering Sir Harry's body on the morning of July 8. But no one could corroborate his testimony. For some jurors and spectators, this was enough to make them wonder just when those bloody fingerprints had been made.

Burns and fingerprints were still the main topic when Captain Edward Melchen took the stand. He explained that he had examined Freddie thoroughly around 7:30 on the evening of July 8. He found a burn on the back of his right hand and forearm, as well as a number of burned hairs. Some had been curled by heat; others had been burned off.

Melchen, a seasoned police veteran, was calm and unruffled throughout the cross-examination, although Godfrey Higgs and his assistant did their best to set him off balance. The most curious part of the questioning revolved around the discovery of Freddie's fingerprint on the screen, which was now referred to as Exhibit J. At one point, Melchen revealed, "I learned about it for the first time when Captain Barker told Lady Oakes the afternoon after Sir Harry's funeral."

Ernest Callender shouted, "During the 36 hours you were travelling together he said nothing to you about the fingerprint?"

"Nothing whatsoever."

The chief justice found this so unusual that he commented upon it in his longhand record of the proceedings. "It is strange that Barker did not tell about the fingerprint," he wrote.

Callender asked whether Melchen thought it appropriate to tell Lady Oakes the gruesome details of Sir Harry's murder so soon after the funeral, suggesting that he and Barker had deliberately done so in order to prejudice her against Freddie. Melchen denied that this was their plan. He also stuck to his story about the singed hairs, as well as his report that Freddie could not produce the shirt he had worn that night. But Higgs presented a different spin on events. Freddie had produced not a single shirt, but several — any one of

Exhibit J

*The fingerprint found on the Chinese screen in Oakes's
bedroom after the murder*

which could have been the shirt in question. He simply could
not tell one from the other.

Despite the shouted questions of both Godfrey Higgs
and Ernest Callender, Melchen got off lightly. Still, in his
cross-examination of the Miami officer, Higgs had raised a
number of provocative points. One had to do with the time at
which Freddie was interviewed at Westbourne on July 9, the
day after the murder. According to Melchen's statement at
the preliminary hearing, Freddie had gone upstairs between
3 and 4 in the afternoon. Two Bahamian police officers had
sworn the same thing. But the diary of Lieutenant John
Douglas, who had guarded Freddie from the late afternoon of

July 8, overnight, and into July 9, showed that he and Freddie had left the mansion between 1:30 and 2 p.m. Melchen backtracked, saying he had made a mistake. It seemed rather strange, observed Ernest Callender, that he and two other constables should make the same mistake. Callender was trying to show that Freddie had been in the room before the investigation began, which would have provided an opportunity for his fingerprint to be applied to the screen several hours after the murder.

How the print had been obtained was also cause for concern. In British Commonwealth courts at the time, photographs of fingerprints were normally accepted as evidence. But this fingerprint had been lifted from the place where it was found, so the defense team argued that it was not admissible evidence.

The chief justice spent the night considering the question of admissibility and decided to leave the matter in the jury's hands. They could consider the evidence, then decide whether it had actually come from the screen. It was a precedent-setting move, the first time that a British court had admitted a lifted print as evidence. When Freddie heard the decision, he shrugged his shoulders and settled back on the bench in the prisoner's cage. Then he smiled. Godfrey Higgs had other strategies up his sleeve and they centred on the younger of the Miami detectives — Captain James Barker.

* * *

Barker was tall, well built, and handsome enough to be a movie detective. That, as any experienced lawyer knew, could persuade jurors to accept his testimony. So Higgs determined to undermine the Miami police officer any way he could. He questioned Barker's qualifications, forcing him to tell how he had been a motorcycle cop, had risen to plainclothes detective, then been demoted for insubordination and subsequently returned to uniform. Although he had since made his way back to being a detective again, eventually becoming superintendent, Higgs's questioning had nonetheless cast a shadow on his reputation.

Higgs then proceeded to attack Barker's competence by questioning the kind of equipment the two detectives had brought with them from Miami. Barker admitted that, although they had expected to look for fingerprints, he did not think to bring a camera. At the time, he was under the impression that he was investigating a suicide. By the time the print was found on the Chinese screen, he and Melchen knew it was murder. Why then, Higgs asked, did they not have a camera flown in from Miami, or borrow one from a commercial photographer in Nassau? Barker admitted he could have done that. The photograph would have preserved an image of the fingerprint where it was found on the Chinese screen.

Higgs was deliberately creating an impression of a careless investigation, of inappropriate actions and tasks left undone. In response to one of Higgs's questions, Barker admitted that there were probably many objects in the room that he did not dust for prints. The reason, he explained, was the nature of the crime. Caught in the grip of emotion, rushing to escape detection, whoever killed Sir Harry would not have handled many items in the room. At least that was Barker's opinion. And yet, Higgs pointed out, Barker had stated that he had dusted several magazines in the bedroom. "Did you think that the assailant was reading books and magazines in Sir Harry's room?" the defense attorney asked.

"I thought he might have touched one," Barker replied.

"What about the headboard?" Higgs asked. Barker replied that he had not dusted it for prints because the heat from the fire would have destroyed latent prints. Higgs wanted to know, then, why Barker would have bothered to examine the screen, which was blistered from the heat of the fire. Barker could provide no satisfactory answer. Nor could he explain why he had chosen not to fingerprint a number of people known to be at Westbourne, including Madeline Kelly, Effie Henneage, Frank Christie, Mabel Ellis, any of the policemen, or the Duke of Windsor. He had accepted at face value statements by others that these individuals had either not been in the bedroom or had not touched anything in the room.

Even more curious was the complete absence of Harold Christie's fingerprints. Barker knew that, shortly after Christie's arrival at the crime scene, he had handled a thermos of water on the bedside table, as well as a glass. Glass was considered an excellent surface for obtaining fingerprints, yet Barker found nothing. Nor did he find other prints in the room, even though Christie had been a frequent visitor and had probably touched several items.

According to Barker, humidity had destroyed many fingerprints. He was "fortunate" to have found Freddie's evidence on the screen, and stated that if he had dusted further, he might have turned up more than a single fingerprint. But he had not dusted further.

"I don't believe 'fortunate' is the word," Higgs commented sarcastically. "Let us say, 'It was a coincidence we found it.'"

At one point, Higgs asked Barker to demonstrate his method of lifting fingerprints. After instructing jurors to place their hands on various surfaces, he showed how fingerprints were lifted with dusting powder and a bit of Scotch tape. Every print he lifted was clear and identifiable. Barker was obviously competent at the procedures he had been describing, and yet his account of his efforts at Westbourne suggested a botched investigation.

Matters went from bad to worse when Higgs, pointing to a blue pencil mark on the screen, asked him whether this was where he had found Freddie's fingerprint. "I cannot definitely say," Barker replied. "But I can say that it came from the top of the panel." He explained that, a week earlier, he and New York fingerprint expert Frank Conway had examined the screen together and could not positively locate the spot where the fingerprint had come from. Nothing seemed to match the photograph.

Higgs probed further, asking when Barker had first marked the screen. The police detective replied that on August 1 he had drawn a black pencil mark around the area, initialled it and written July 9 — the day after Sir Harry's body was discovered.

"Then, until August 1, there was nothing on the screen to indicate where the print came from?" Higgs asked.

"Nothing but my memory," Barker replied.

Higgs proceeded to refresh Barker's memory further, noting that on the third of August, in magistrate's court, the detective had sworn that he had previously marked the spot with a black pencil. While in magistrate's court that day, he circled it with a blue pencil, initialled it, and dated it 8-3-43.

"You marked this area in blue in Magistrate's Court and said that this is where the print came from?" asked Higgs.

Barker admitted that he had.

"Why?"

"I am not sure now."

Higgs suggested that Leonard Keeler, the investigator who was assisting with Freddie's defense, had indicated that the print could not possibly have come from the area circled in blue. Any print lifted from that area would have shown some of the decorative scrollwork — but Exhibit J showed none. That, he argued, was why Barker was now changing his testimony, claiming he was not certain where the fingerprint had been found.

Then Higgs directed himself to Sir Oscar, the chief justice, saying that the defense had been "taken completely by surprise" by the shifting location of the fingerprints. He requested permission to look at the screen once more and to ask Barker additional questions.

Sir Oscar agreed.

Higgs asked Barker if surface markings, such as the ornate decoration on the screen, would show in a lifted print. Barker conceded that they could. "Then why were they not visible in the photo?" asked Higgs.

"Because it was lifted from a part of the surface where no irregularities would show."

Having established that the piece of adhesive that Barker had used to lift the print measured 1 by 3 inches, Higgs invited the detective to show such a spot on the screen. The Miami cop crossed the room to the screen. His face was flushed, his gestures uncertain. He waved his hand toward several places where the fingerprint might have been located.

Sir Oscar, who had joined Higgs and Barker beside the screen, told him to take his time.

Higgs pushed harder. Finally, Sir Oscar adjourned the court.

The adjournment gave Barker some breathing room, but only temporarily. Higgs was back in action the next day, October 31. During his cross-examination, he took Barker back to the day Melchen had taken Freddie upstairs at

Westbourne to question him.

"Did you go to the door of the room and ask Melchen if everything was OK?"

"I did not."

"Wasn't Exhibit J taken from some object in that room?"

"Definitely not."

"I suggest you and Captain Melchen definitely planned to get the accused alone to get his fingerprint."

"No, sir."

"I suggest Exhibit J never came from that screen."

"It came from Panel Five on that screen."

"This is an outstanding case in which your expert assistance is required?"

"It developed that way."

"I suggest that in your desire for gain and notoriety, you have swept aside the truth and substituted fabricated evidence."

"That is untrue."

Yet repeated attempts had failed to locate a part of the screen where a fingerprint could be lifted without some trace of the ornate pattern showing.

When Higgs was finally done with Barker, Hallinan took over. The attorney general led Barker through testimony in which the Miami policeman had removed the print for fear that it would be damaged if left on the screen.

On November 1, Frank Conway took the stand. The New York fingerprint expert confirmed that Exhibit J came from the little finger of Freddie de Marigny's right hand. Godfrey Higgs told the court that the defense was not arguing that fact.

Much of the questioning focussed on standard practice by fingerprint experts. Conway testified that lifting prints was acceptable, especially if there was a chance they might be destroyed. However, he said that if *he* had been called to investigate, he would not have arrived in Nassau without his fingerprint camera, and, furthermore, in his experience, objects carrying prints were usually brought into court. He also explained that prints were usually circled on the object on which they were found. If there was more than one print, each print was circled and numbered. If the prints were lifted, the photographs of the lifted prints were numbered correspondingly.

Then the defense team sent Conway to the screen and asked if he could see anywhere prints might have been lifted. Conway said there were traces of three lifts. If Exhibit J had come from the area Barker had indicated, it would have "come pretty close" to the decorative scrollwork on the screen. In fact, he said, if Exhibit J was pressed on the screen, the scrollwork would probably show, especially if the area was soiled. The screen, of course, had been soiled by soot generated by the fire.

The technical details may have confused the jurors, and Sir Oscar as well. At one point, the chief justice asked Conway directly where the fingerprint had been taken from the screen. "I cannot say where," the fingerprint expert stated.

By the time the discussion of fingerprints was over, it seemed Freddie's chance of an acquittal had improved. But then testimony turned to the matter of his finances. Bank accountant Lewis Phillips revealed that, the day before Sir Harry's murder, Freddie's account was overdrawn by £57. Reviewing other records, he testified that, soon after marrying Nancy, Freddie had paid £7,000 to his cousin Georges, and in April 1943 Nancy had cabled £3,000 to Else de Marigny, Freddie's mother, in Mauritius. Phillips also indicated that Nancy spent "large sums" after she and Freddie were married.

As everyone who had followed the trial was aware, Freddie enjoyed a lavish lifestyle. When John H. Anderson, the bank manager who had told Freddie about Sir Harry's death, took the stand, he reported that Freddie had spent more than $100,000 of Ruth's money. According to Anderson, Freddie had given him detailed information about his financial situation in June, when he said that, aside from some property, he had "spent his last cent."

The financial information was only part of Anderson's testimony. Anderson had driven Freddie out to the Kelly cottage after telling him about Sir Harry's death. Now, he was asked to describe that journey, Freddie's 15-minute absence and his comments about Sir Harry's murder when he returned. As far as the Crown was concerned, Freddie knew far more than he could possibly have learned by talking to anyone at the estate. However, the defense suggested that Freddie might have had time to get into the room — a

Exhibit J

possibility that was made more probable when police corporal Cleophas Knowles testified under cross-examination that he had left his post on the second floor of Westbourne for a few moments.

No one seemed to take into account that Freddie was on good terms with many members of Sir Harry's staff and could have received a detailed description of Sir Harry's body and bedroom from them.

As a bank manager, John Anderson was a credible witness. But his testimony also revealed how even the most seemingly respectable members of Nassau society could be operating outside the law. On the day of Freddie's arrest, Anderson had helped remove seven 50-gallon drums of gasoline from the de Marigny house. Having that quantity of gasoline was against rationing laws, and by helping Freddie, Anderson was breaking the law. He had been aware of this, and he had still helped. However, once the news of the murder was announced, he decided to make a statement to police.

On Wednesday, November 3, Lady Oakes took the stand, again reiterating the hostility between her husband and her son-in-law. By now, everyone was familiar with the details. She finished shortly after 3 p.m. At 3:18, Eric Hallinan rose. "That is the Crown's case, Your Honour," he stated.

Chapter 8
Verdict

hile the defense prepared to present their version of events, Sir Oscar turned to Freddie de Marigny. As the defendant, he had three choices, the chief justice explained. He could remain silent. He could give an unsworn statement from the prisoner's dock, which would form part of the official record. Or he could testify under oath — but if he did so, he would be subject to cross-examination.

Freddie didn't hesitate. "I will testify," he said in a clear, loud voice. He was on his feet, ready to leave the prisoner's pen for the witness stand. At that moment, Sir Oscar decided it was time to adjourn for the day.

On Thursday, November 4, Freddie de Marigny took the

stand. His expression was grim, but his voice was steady and confident, as he answered questions about the night of the murder. Just as Lady Eunice had done the day before, Freddie recounted his version of the relationship with Sir Harry. In one quarrel, Freddie recalled, Sir Harry had referred to Nancy as "that girl in your house," complaining that she had caused her mother more than enough trouble and that he wanted nothing more to do with her. Nancy would get nothing from him. Freddie said he emphasized the point by spelling out the word, twice, loudly, "N-O-T-H-I-N-G."

Freddie also spoke about the quarrel in the hospital in Florida. He had threatened to "knock Sir Harry out of the room" if he bothered Nancy during her recuperation. He had quarrelled with the surgeon, Dr. William Sayad, about whether or not Nancy's parents should be allowed to visit.

As he had repeated numerous times previously, he was home in bed when Sir Harry was killed. He had wakened during the night when Grisou, his cousin Georges's cat, had fought with Freddie's dog. He recounted the trip with John Anderson to the Newell Kelly cottage, and how he had walked over to Westbourne and learned from conversations there the details of Sir Harry's death.

Finally, Godfrey Higgs asked if Freddie had gone to Westbourne around the time of the murder.

"I did not," Freddie replied firmly.

"Did you kill Sir Harry Oakes?"

Freddie raised his head, eyes flashing. "No sir! No, sir!"

* * *

Eric Hallinan handled the cross-examination, which began the next day. The attorney general pushed hard, but Freddie remained calm. One line of questioning focussed on a trip to California with another couple. This was before Freddie and Nancy married, and the prosecution emphasized the fact that, although the other female member of the foursome was a married woman, she was still in her teens and hardly a suitable chaperone. Hallinan also asked Freddie about spending Ruth's money. Freddie insisted he had funded the California trip with his own money.

Other questions focussed on his failed relationship with Ruth and the circumstances that led to Freddie's marriage to Nancy. The prosecution's line of questioning was designed to portray Freddie as a gigolo, a man who accepted money from women and preyed on innocent young girls like Nancy Oakes.

Then it was back to the relationship with his father-in-law. Freddie was cool when Hallinan asked if he felt angry or humiliated by Sir Harry's treatment. Freddie said that he didn't. "I knew he had a violent temper and easily lost it."

Again and again, in his answers to the attorney general, Freddie created a portrait of Sir Harry as a volatile, irascible father-in-law, and of himself struggling to tolerate an unreasonable man. Had Freddie been angry at the accusation that he was a sex maniac, Hallinan asked. "Not as he shouted it. I might have had he spoken it coolly."

Godfrey Higgs then called to the witness stand two more people who had attended Freddie's dinner party the night of the murder. Both Donald McKinney and Oswald Mosely testified that they had seen Freddie light the hurricane lamp, putting his hand in the shade as he did so and being burned in the process.

The defense called Betty Roberts, Georges Visdelou's 17-year-old girlfriend. After the dinner party, she testified, the two of them had gone upstairs. They had fallen asleep — Georges on the bed, Betty on the couch. About 1:30 a.m., someone knocked on the door. It was Freddie. He and Georges conversed in French for a few moments, then Freddie offered to drive Betty home. She turned down the invitation. When Freddie left, she and Georges fell asleep again. When she next woke, it was 2:40 a.m. She woke Georges and they went downstairs. Georges's car was not where it had been parked earlier, but was behind the house. Freddie would have had to move it to drive his female guests home. Betty recalled that at 3:15 Georges drove her home.

Likely, no one believed Betty's testimony about the sleeping arrangements, but the rest of her story seemed credible. When Georges testified, however, there were problems. Adderley produced a statement that Georges had given to the police. In it, he claimed he had not seen his cousin from midnight, after the dinner party, until 3:15 a.m., when he was asked to move the troublesome car. Georges explained his confusion by saying he was nervous. "I am French and very emotional," he added.

Yet he had managed to recall many details about his early life in Mauritius, and later in London, England. Why could he do this, and not recall information about a more recent event, Sir Oscar asked. Georges was unable to offer a reasonable explanation.

Fortunately, Higgs came to the rescue by reading a portion of the same statement, which Adderley had deliberately skipped. In this section, Georges had stated that Freddie had come to the apartment about 1:30 to ask to drive Betty home. Obviously he was confused at the time he had made the statement, not making changes in order to save his cousin now that the trial was underway.

Two more witnesses contradicted the prosecution's physical evidence. Dr. Ulrich Oberwarth, the prison physician who had examined Freddie at the time of his arrest, swore there were no burned hairs on Freddie's body when he examined him. And perhaps the most dramatic testimony of the day came from Captain Maurice B. O'Neill of the New Orleans police. "I can say positively that Exhibit J did not come from that screen," O'Neill testified. He demonstrated by having jury foreman James Sands put his finger on a clean glass ashtray, then lifting off the print. Clearly visible were circles that were part of the shape of the glass. If such details could be picked up from a glass, surely the ornate decoration on the Chinese screen should have been visible when Freddie's print was lifted from it.

One man who was notably absent was Police Commissioner Erskine-Lindop. Although Godfrey Higgs chose not to focus on the information, Freddie claimed he had been in Sir Harry's room after the murder was reported *and Erskine-Lindop could confirm this*. But Erskine-Lindop had been abruptly transferred to another posting before the trial began and, for reasons that were never explained, no one had thought to take a statement from him.

The final witness was Nancy de Marigny. When she took the stand, she seemed very young, tense, and vulnerable. As she answered questions, Freddie began to weep silently in the prisoner's pen. It was the first time he had broken down during the trial, and it did not last long. With considerable effort, he managed to get himself under control. Some time later, when Nancy seemed on the verge of tears, he was able to give her an encouraging look.

Nancy went to great lengths to describe the circumstances of her pregnancy, including the timing, to make it clear that Freddie had not insisted on marital relations before she was fully recovered from typhoid. In fact, Nancy said, her doctors had advised her to "live normally" while she recuperated.

The hardest part was the discussion of her father's death, and how Captain Barker had described Sir Harry's last hours in vivid detail. Hallinan wisely avoided putting Nancy through more painful recollections. Instead, his cross-examination focussed primarily on a letter written by her to her parents, asking them to accept Freddie as part of the family. Nancy accused them both of being unreasonable, of listening to rumours. "If you and father cannot accept my husband and give him the trust and respect due him, then there is no question where my decision lies," she wrote. Nancy would choose her husband over her parents and refuse to have anything more to do with them.

When Hallinan asked if she meant to make good on the threat, she said, "I probably would have, unless they changed their attitudes, which I hoped they would do."

Nancy was the last witness called. The contents of the letter and who was behind it was one of the key points in Hallinan's summation. "Does this sound like a letter written by a girl of 19?" Hallinan asked the jury. "It sounds like a man saying, 'If I can't be with Nancy, I'll cut her off from her family.' It's a gambler's throw." He portrayed Freddie as someone so desperate for money that he was willing to resort to murder.

In contrast, Higgs's summation stressed the circumstantial nature of the evidence, and, most importantly, the problems with the testimony and evidence presented by the two Miami police officers. The testimony against the accused, he said, was "a combination of statements of an irrelevant nature and deliberate lying by police officers, whose duty is to protect the public."

Sir Oscar Daly spent more than five hours in his charge to the jury. "There is no halfway measure in this case," he warned. "Your duty is to find the accused guilty or not. There is no evidence here of manslaughter or killing in self-defense.

If the evidence shows the accused committed the crime, you must find him guilty. Likewise, it is your solemn duty to give him the benefit of the doubt."

He reviewed the evidence, providing the legal guidance he felt the jury required. Not surprisingly, a considerable portion of his discussion centred on the fingerprints. While Daly dismissed Higgs's accusations that the evidence had been fabricated, he did make it clear that there were serious flaws in Barker's testimony, including several extraordinary lapses of memory and his inability to pinpoint the location where the fingerprint was found on the screen.

Before the chief justice finished speaking, Nancy slipped quietly out of the courtroom. When the jury retired, Freddie was escorted to the police station. He was smiling as he walked the short distance along Nassau's main street.

It took just 1 hour and 40 minutes for the jury to decide Freddie's fate. By 7:10 that evening, everyone was back in the courtroom. Nancy had chosen a spot near the door, ready for a quick exit. Everyone was talking at once as the jury filed in.

At 7:15, guards stationed in the courtroom called for silence. Sir Oscar addressed the jury. James Sands, the jury foreman, rose. A guard lifted the heavy lid from the prisoner's pen, and Freddie stood up. Sir Oscar asked the question: "How do you find the accused?"

"Not guilty, nine to three," James Sands began.

The courtroom erupted with cheers. Amid the bedlam, Sir Oscar ordered Freddie released. Freddie burst out of the prisoner's pen and ran to Nancy. They embraced, then moved quickly through the door and into a waiting car. Meanwhile, order had been restored and the jury foreman continued.

The jury had found Freddie de Marigny not guilty of murder. Nevertheless, all 12 members were unanimous in recommending his immediate deportation from the Bahamas.

Although the recommendation had no legal standing, Sir Oscar said that he would pass it on to the appropriate authorities.

Chapter 9
Aftermath

Baroness Marie af Trolle, an old school chum of Nancy Oakes de Marigny, celebrated Freddie's acquittal by hosting a party in his honour. Among the many guests were private detective Raymond Schindler and Leonard Keeler, head of the first police crime lab in the United States and a pioneer in the use of the polygraph, or lie detector. During the evening, Keeler entertained guests by having several of them pick a card from a deck, show it to others, then either tell the truth or lie to him about which card it was while he checked their reaction on the polygraph. Without fail, he was able to catch the guests who failed to tell the truth.

Then Freddie suddenly asked to be tested. Nancy looked

worried, and Keeler was also concerned about administering the test with so many people watching. He realized the problems that would be created if Freddie failed the test, or if the results were ambiguous. But Freddie was insistent. "Ask me anything about the case," he said. "Just don't ask me anything about my past."

At least three times, Keeler asked Freddie if he had killed Harry Oakes. Each time, Freddie emphatically denied it — and the machine indicated he was telling the truth.

Nevertheless, Freddie's innocence was no protection from the vindictiveness of the Bahamian establishment. During Prohibition, when too many people with mob connections were settling in the islands, the government had passed legislation that allowed deportation of any "undesirable" non-Bahamian. No formal charge was required, no trial was necessary and no appeal was allowed.

Two days after Freddie's acquittal, the Governor-in-Council issued the decree. The Duke of Windsor was still away, as he had been since before the murder trial began, and Leslie Heape, the colonial secretary, acted in his place. Freddie and his cousin Georges were "invited" to leave because of "moral turpitude" and the violation of exchange regulations. Godfrey Higgs argued strongly against the order, but lost.

The Bahamian government could not immediately put the order into effect, however. Because of the war, it was impossible to send Freddie back to Mauritius. As a British citizen, he might have tried to go to England, but transatlantic travel was still difficult. In addition, because the United States would not grant him a visa, Pan Am refused to allow him to board an airplane.

When the Duke and Duchess of Windsor returned from several weeks' vacation, Freddie was still in Nassau. Almost immediately, Edward began working behind the scenes, contacting the British government directly to enlist their support to throw Freddie out of the Bahamas. In one cablegram, he said that Freddie "has evil reputation for immoral conduct with young girls. Is gambler and spendthrift. Suspected drug addict."

Finally, Cuban officials offered to allow Freddie into the country. He and Nancy spent some time with writer Ernest Hemingway, whom Freddie had met onboard ship during his first voyage to the United States. But Cuba's humid climate did not agree with Nancy. When she needed yet another operation, she left for Vermont.

Determined to join his wife, Freddie found himself a job on a merchant ship sailing for Halifax. At first, Canadian officials refused to permit him to enter the country. Then his ship went into dry dock for repairs and he was granted a 30-day visa. He rushed to Montreal to meet Nancy, but the reunion was a disaster. She was involved with another man. In retrospect, Freddie wrote years later, the devotion she had shown during the trial may have come more from a desire to be in the spotlight than from any deep affection.

At Nancy's insistence, and despite Freddie's efforts to stop it, the marriage was annulled. Before Nancy could marry Joergen Edsberg, the Danish airman for whom she had left Freddie, Edsberg was killed. Thereafter, she was frequently seen in the company of movie stars and other celebrities and did eventually marry twice more, but both marriages ended in divorce. Nancy died in London, England, in January 2005.

Denied permanent residency in Canada, Freddie drifted back to Cuba, lived in Mexico for a time, and eventually settled in the United States. He also remarried and raised a family, and in 1975 renounced his aristocratic title to become an American citizen. In 1990, his biography, including his version of the Oakes trial, was published. Freddie died in Houston, Texas, on January 28, 1998.

The Duke of Windsor resigned as governor of the Bahamas in early 1945, several months before his term was up. He never again held a responsible post and died in a Paris hospital in 1972.

James Barker's mishandling of the fingerprint evidence in the Oakes case led to an investigation following his return to Miami. When it was over, Barker was placed on indefinite sick leave. He became a drug addict and grew increasingly violent. On December 26, 1952, he threatened his son with a .38 revolver. The son, who was also a police officer, struggled with his father and the gun discharged. James Barker died instantly. It was later revealed that for several years Barker had been taking payment from the mob.

Meanwhile, Harold Christie's plans for developing the Bahamas as a tourist attraction were bearing fruit. The casino he had dreamed of for so long was finally built, and the money began flowing into the islands. Christie became very wealthy and was highly respected for his honesty and integrity. He was knighted in 1964 and died of a heart attack in 1973.

* * *

In 1944, the year after Freddie de Marigny was acquitted, Raymond Schindler tried to reopen the case. He wrote to the Duke of Windsor, who, in his capacity as Governor General of the Bahamas, had the power to authorize this. The letter was acknowledged, but no action was taken.

The case was referred to New Scotland Yard in 1947. Again, little action was taken. In May 1959, the Bahamian House of Assembly passed a resolution, asking that the case be reopened. Raymond Schindler was contacted and asked to provide any evidence he had available. Before he could comply, he suffered a fatal heart attack.

Aside from Freddie de Marigny, no other suspect was ever arrested for the murder of Sir Harry Oakes. Many writers, however, have concluded that Freddie was a scapegoat who was deliberately singled out because he was an outsider who had repeatedly irritated authorities. Freddie's driver and right-hand man, George Thompson, was beaten by police in an effort to force him to say that he had driven Freddie to Westbourne on the night of the murder. Some of Freddie's friends were strongly advised not to testify on his behalf, or were asked if they were being paid to provide him with an alibi. Police Commissioner Erskine-Lindop was prevented from carrying out the investigation, then pushed out of the picture completely with a transfer to Trinidad. And, although it was never proven in court, the evidence presented strongly suggested that Exhibit J, the fingerprint Barker had discovered at the crime scene, had been planted to incriminate Freddie de Marigny.

The case remains officially unsolved, but two questions remain. Who killed Sir Harry Oakes? And why?

Epilogue
Who Killed Harry Oakes?

othing is more tantalizing than an unsolved mystery. Over the years, many explanations have been offered about the murder. The most dramatic explanation suggests that Sir Harry Oakes was killed by the mob.

Rumours were fueled by reports of a mysterious yacht that appeared off the coast of Nassau shortly before Sir Harry's death and disappeared almost as quickly as it had arrived. Harold Christie had ties to the mob, as did James Barker. Meyer Lansky, one of the Mafia kingpins controlling gambling and organized crime, was eager to see casinos established in the Bahamas.

One scenario suggests that Harold Christie had

persuaded both the Duke of Windsor and Sir Harry Oakes to support the introduction of casinos. With their combined influence and power, they could have the laws against gambling changed. They could all reap profits, as well as move money about in spite of currency restrictions. Then, the theory goes, Sir Harry backed out, perhaps because he realized how dramatically the little paradise he had come to love would change with the arrival of casinos.

Sir Harry Oakes was a stubborn man. Once he made up his mind, there was little that could be done to change it. But he was dealing with powerful and violent individuals. On the night of the murder, during the wild storm that kept almost everyone indoors, Harold Christie had driven him to the dock for a clandestine rendezvous aboard the mystery yacht. When Sir Harry would not change his mind, he was either deliberately killed, or beaten as a warning, dying of his injuries. Then someone drove Harold Christie back to Westbourne and tried to make the murder look like an accident. The next day, Christie revealed some of the details to the Duke of Windsor, who set in motion a chain of events designed to prevent investigators from uncovering the truth.

But there is another interpretation of events, one that is less melodramatic but far more sordid. While the Duke of Windsor was singularly incompetent in many of his undertakings, Harold Christie was not. Christie also had mob connections. It was known that Christie had spent considerable sums of his own and Sir Harry's money in real estate and tourist development. Despite his reputation for honesty, Christie might have taken too many liberties with Sir Harry's money. Sir Harry had a reputation for vindictiveness and had exposed dishonest partners in the past. Perhaps, the two men had gone to a business meeting on the yacht. Perhaps Sir Harry had been driving the station wagon when Captain Sears saw it in downtown Nassau. And perhaps, once back at Westbourne, the two men had quarrelled. Harold Christie, some 20 years younger than Sir Harry, had struck and killed him. Then, with the aid of the Duke of Windsor, he concocted a cover story.

Edward may have been nothing more than an unwitting dupe acting upon Christie's suggestions. But the total absence of Christie's fingerprints at the crime scene and the deliberate destruction of bloody handprints and fingerprints attests to a cover-up designed to protect one man: Harold Christie.

Appendix
Cast of Characters

Alfred Adderley – Crown prosecutor in the Oakes murder case

James Barker – Miami police captain, part of team brought in to investigate the murder

Ernest Callender – Assistant attorney for defense in the Oakes murder case

Harold Christie – Bahamian real estate dealer and Sir Harry's business partner

John Douglas – Bahamian police officer who guarded Freddie de Marigny prior to arrest

R. A. Erskine-Lindop – Bahamian police commissioner

Eric Hallinan – Attorney General of the Bahamas

Godfrey Higgs – Defense attorney in the Oakes murder case

Leonard Keeler – Fingerprint and polygraph expert assisting Raymond Schindler

Freddie de Marigny – Aristocratic playboy who eloped with Nancy Oakes

Edward Melchen – Miami police captain assisting James Barker in the murder investigation

Appendix

Lady Eunice Oakes – Sir Harry's Australian-born wife

Sir Harry Oakes – Millionaire miner who moved to the Bahamas from Canada

Nancy Oakes – Sir Harry's eldest daughter

Ruth Fahnestock Schermerhorn – Ex-wife of Freddie de Marigny

Raymond Schindler – Famous American detective hired by Nancy Oakes de Marigny to conduct a separate investigation of the crime

Edward Sears – Captain in Bahamian police department and childhood chum of Harold Christie

Georges de Visdelou – Cousin and close friend of Freddie de Marigny

Duchess of Windsor – Former Wallis Warfield Simpson, the American divorcée for whom Edward VIII gave up his throne

Edward, Duke of Windsor – Governor General of the Bahamas and ex–king Edward VIII of England

Acknowledgments

The author acknowledges the following sources, portions of which have been quoted in this book: *The Life and Death of Sir Harry Oakes* by Geoffrey Bocca; *A Conspiracy of Crowns* by Alfred de Marigny; *Who Killed Sir Harry Oakes?* by Marshall Houtts; *Who Killed Sir Harry Oakes?* by James Leasor; "The Murdered Midas of Lake Shore" by Barbara Moon in *Maclean's* Magazine, September 1, 1950; *Time Magazine*; *Newsweek*; and the *New York Times*.

Thanks also go to editors Frances Purslow and Marial Shea for their many suggestions and close attention to detail.

Further Reading

Bocca, Geoffrey. *The Life and Death of Sir Harry Oakes.* London: Weidenfeld & Nicolson, 1959.

De Marigny, Alfred. *A Conspiracy of Crowns.* New York: Crown Publishers Inc., 1990.

Leasor, James. *Who Killed Sir Harry Oakes?* Boston: Houghton Mifflin Company, 1983.

Parker, John. *King of Fools.* New York: St. Martin's Press, 1988.

About the Author

Cheryl MacDonald has been writing about Canadian history for more than 30 years. A former Montrealer and long-time resident of Nanticoke, Ontario, she is a full-time writer and historian whose weekly history column appears in the *Simcoe Times-Reformer*. Her historical articles have appeared in *The Beaver*, *Maclean's*, the *Hamilton Spectator*, and *The Old Farmer's Almanac*.

Cheryl has also written or co-authored more than 30 books on Canadian and Ontario history, including Amazing Stories titles *Niagara Daredevils*, *Deadly Women of Ontario*, and *Celebrated Pets*.

A member of both the Professional Writers Association of Canada and Crime Writers of Canada, Cheryl has a master's degree in history from McMaster University, Hamilton and is an enthusiastic historical re-enactor with a special interest in the War of 1812. Contact her through her Web site: www.heronwoodent.ca.

Points of Interest

Museum of Northern History, Kirkland Lake, Ontario. Formerly Harry Oakes's chateau, located close to Lake Shore mine. 2 Chateau Drive, Kirkland Lake.

www.town.kirklandlake.on.ca/museum.html

Oakes Garden Theatre, Niagara Falls, Ontario. Park financed by Harry Oakes during his time in Niagara Falls.

www.niagaraparks.com/aboutus/wedding.php

Oak Hall, Niagara Falls, Ontario. Harry Oakes's residence from 1928 until his move to the Bahamas in 1934. Although now the administrative headquarters of the Niagara Parks Commission, portions of the building are open to the public.

www.niagaraparks.com/aboutus/oakhall.php

Index

Index

Murder!

Murder!